A
COASTAL
DIARY

John Landy

A Coastal Diary

A Study Of One Of Australia's Wildest And Most Beautiful Coastlines

MACMILLAN
AUSTRALIA

TITLE PAGE: Cape Otway lighthouse, from Point Franklin.
ACKNOWLEDGEMENTS: Sunrise over Jarosite Headland.

First published 1993 by Pan Macmillan Publishers Australia
a division of Pan Macmillan Australia Pty Limited
63-71 Balfour Street, Chippendale, Sydney
A.C.N. 001 184 014

National Library of Australia
cataloguing-in-publication data:

Landy, John, 1930–
A coastal diary.
Bibliography.
Includes index.
ISBN 0 7329 0773 X.

1. Natural history—Victoria. 2. Natural history—New South
Wales.
3. Coasts—Victoria. 4. Coasts—New South Wales. I. Title.
508.944

Typeset in 11/12 pt Bembo by Midland Typesetters,
Maryborough, Victoria 3465.
Printed in Singapore by Kyodo Printing

CONTENTS

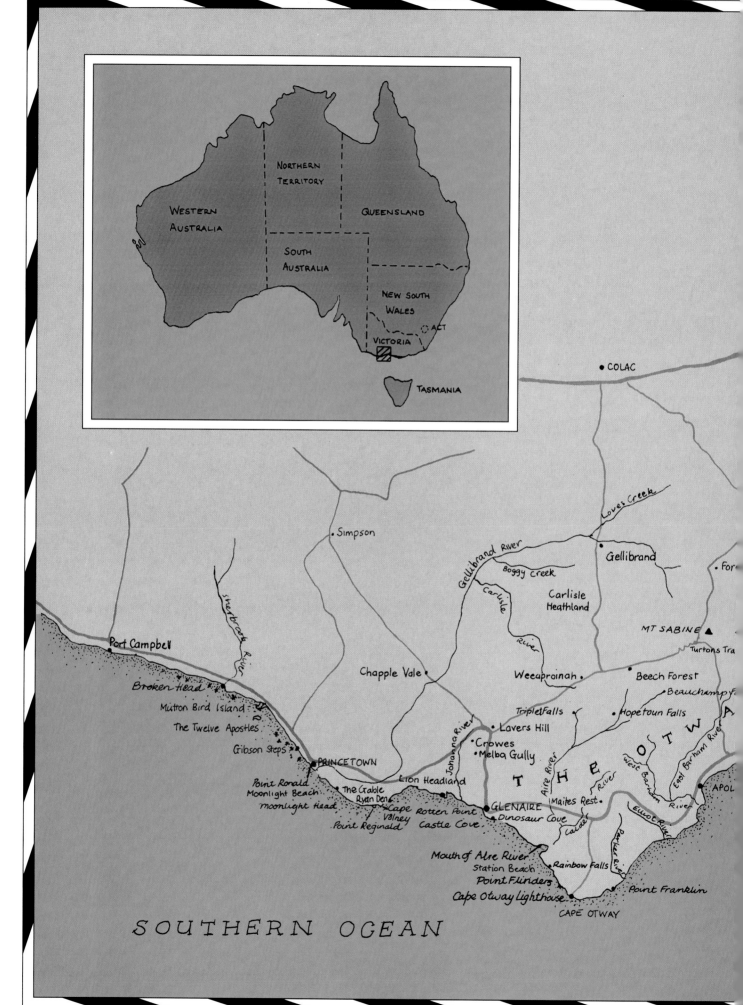

NORTHERN
TERRITORY

WESTERN
AUSTRALIA

QUEENSLAND

SOUTH
AUSTRALIA

NEW SOUTH
WALES

• ACT

VICTORIA

TASMANIA

• COLAC

Loves Creek

• Simpson

Gellibrand River

Boggy Creek

• Gellibrand

• For

Carlisle

Carlisle
Heathland

MT SABINE ▲

Sherbrook River

River

Turtons Tra

Port Campbell

Chapple Vale •

Weeaproinah •

• Beech Forest

Broken Head

• Beauchamp f.

Mutton Bird Island

Triplet Falls

• Hopetoun Falls

The Twelve Apostles

Johanna River

• Lavers Hill

T H E   O T W A

Gibson Steps

• Crowes
• Melba Gully

PRINCETOWN

Lion Headland

Aire River

River

West Barham River

East Barham River

APOL

Point Ronald
Moonlight Beach

The Crable
Ryan Den

Cape
Volney

Rotten Point

GLENAIRE
• Dinosaur Cove

Maites Rest •

Elliot River

moonlight Head

Castle Cove •

Calder

Parker R.

Point Reginald

Mouth of Aire River
Station Beach
Point Flinders

• Rainbow Falls

• Point Franklin

Cape Otway Lighthouse

CAPE OTWAY

SOUTHERN   OCEAN

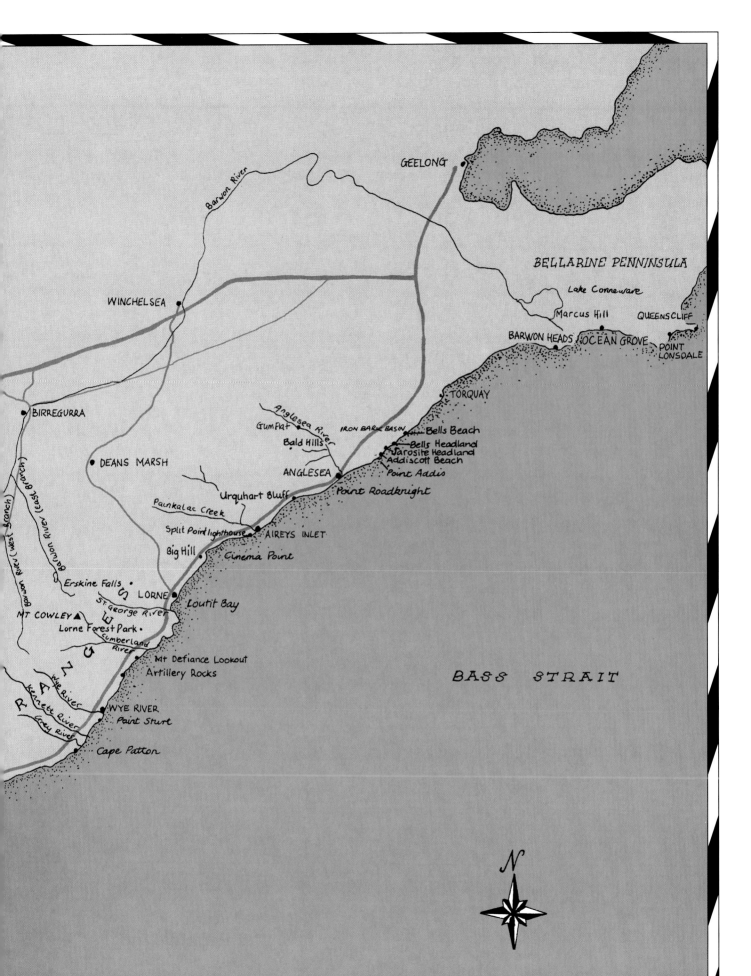

ACKNOWLEDGEMENTS

For this project I have had a great deal of help from many people.

I am particularly indebted to Mary White. Mary, who was born near Apollo Bay, is a legend in the Anglesea district both for her unrivalled knowledge of local natural history and for her selfless and untiring work to interest people in the environment and to preserve what remains of this wonderful area at a time of intense coastal development. I had many discussions with Mary and she located several of the plants that appear as photographs in this book.

Dr Jack Douglas, formerly Principal Research Geologist for the State of Victoria, gave most generously of his time to check my notes on matters geological and palaeontological. He was also able to advise on more general aspects of the Otways, since he spent some of his early years at Lavers Hill and has maintained a very close interest in the district ever since.

I am very grateful to Dr Ebbe Nielsen and to Ted Edwards of the Division of Entomology, CSIRO, Canberra, and to other staff of the Division who identified slides and provided information on insect biology. Other entomologists who helped with my enquiries were Ken Walker of the Museum of Victoria and Dr Dan Bickel and Max Moulds of the Australian Museum, Sydney. Dr Bryan Barlow, Dr Tony Brown and Dr Jeremy Burdon of the Division of Plant Industry, CSIRO, helped me with my enquiries about plant biology.

Spiders, never an easy subject on which to find answers, was handled for me by Dr Robert Raven of the Queensland Museum.

Dr Margaret Clayton of Monash University was most helpful in identifying seaweeds and locating papers on aspects about which I needed information.

The staff of the National Herbarium, Melbourne, particularly Dr Tom May on fungi and David Albrecht on vascular plants, assisted with identifications and in answering questions about distribution. Well-known botanist and conservationist Dr Malcolm Calder, who has helped me readily in the past, again assisted with several of my enquiries and pointed me in new directions regarding things I should look for in my wanderings.

I spent a couple of most interesting days with Dr Tom Rich and his dedicated and enthusiastic team at Dinosaur Cove and learned about his quest to discover the nature of the dinosaurs and their environment which existed over 100 million years ago. Elizabeth Thompson, a member of Tom's staff located at the Museum of Melbourne, was most helpful in providing me with papers on the subject of the dinosaur. Another member of the museum staff, Sue Boyd, provided great assistance with the identification of molluscs and with information on their biology, and Rory O'Brien answered some queries concerning birds.

In writing this book I had valuable discussions with Dr Eric Bird, a world authority on coastal geomorphology, particularly in relation to the disappearance of beaches along our coastline.

David Clark of the Victorian Archaeological Survey was very helpful in providing me with papers and advice on the Aboriginal history of the Otways.

Historian Jane Lennon of the Department of Conservation and Natural Resources located several valuable documents for me and advised me where to seek further information.

On the local scene, the late Percy Hampshire of Johanna River, whose family arrived at Johanna Beach in 1888 on the ketch *Emily* and survived a hazardous landing in which the boat was subsequently wrecked, provided some most interesting insights into the early days of the district. Two other farmers at Johanna, Wayne Robertson and Colin Douglas, discussed farming problems and identified local features that were worth examining. Bill Bowker, who farms at Princetown on a property which his family took up in the 1850s, provided valuable background on this part of the coastline. Paul Millar of the Department of Conservation and Natural Resources gave me another perspective of the Otway forests when he led a party, including myself, to see some big trees near Apollo Bay. Dr John Piesse, an outstanding photographer who accompanied me on that memorable trip, also led me into some very remote parts of the Otways that I would otherwise not have seen.

Some very useful and interesting background on the history of local beaches was provided by my brother-in-law Garth Manton and by John Laird, both long-time Anglesea identities.

I found several books invaluable and would recommend them to anyone wishing to follow up topics briefly discussed by me—firstly, the late Professor WJ Dakin's classic book *Australian Seashores*, which has been splendidly revised and illustrated by one of the original coauthors, Isobel Bennett. For matters on trees and shrubs, Leon Costermans' book *Native Trees and Shrubs of South Eastern Australia* is most comprehensive and easy to use. Mary White's *The Flowers of the Anglesea River Valley* must be the easiest book ever written to help the layman track down the identity of a wildflower, and Jean Galbraith's classic work *Wildflowers of South-East Australia* is a 'must' for me wherever I go in the bush. Jack Loney's several histories covering the region are excellent, and Norm Houghton has covered the history of the timber railways and tramways in a number of highly readable books and articles. There is also a very well illustrated natural history of the area entitled *The Otways*, written by Geelong naturalist Trevor Pescott and published in 1976.

Not so easily accessible are numerous papers on a variety of subjects relating to this district, including geology, coastal geomorphology and the effects of fire, by the late Edmund Gill, a former Deputy Director of the Museum of Victoria. I found them very interesting and highly readable and reference is made to them in the bibliography.

Although I took all the photographs in this book, the subject matter for five was provided for me and they were not taken *in situ*. Jack Douglas loaned me better examples of the fossil fern leaves and the nodules on the roots of an ancient conifer than I was able to locate myself. He also provided me with a tektite he found on the Rivernook Track years ago, a locality I searched diligently but unfruitfully for these elusive objects from outer space. Tom Rich kindly allowed me to photograph the dinosaur skull from the Museum of Victoria collection.

In the actual writing of this diary I would like to thank Kaye Hansen who found many of the references for me when I was too busy doing other things, and Diane Fitt and Margot Kiddle who did the typing.

Finally, I am most indebted to Julia Stiles for her dedicated and meticulous editing, to April Briscoe for the layout of photographs, and to Hilary McPhee for so enthusiastically supporting the idea that my diary notes become a book.

JOHN LANDY
1993

INTRODUCTION

I have always been fascinated by the Australian coastline – the diverse plant and animal life, the moods of the sea, the storms, the sunrise on lines of surf, and the ebb and flow of the tide – and I wanted to record what I could of this varying landscape. So, late in 1986 I began a study of one of Australia's wildest and most beautiful coastal areas – the Otways.

Lying close to the most southern part of the Australian continent, the Otway ranges run for over 80 kilometres in a southwest direction roughly parallel to the coast. Near Olangolah, they divide, the Seaview Ridge running gently southward to Cape Otway and the main ridge following a longer path southwest to Moonlight Head. The Otways spawn a series of short, fast-flowing streams along their seaward scarp, each broken at intervals by waterfalls and rapids before it reaches the ocean. On the inward-facing edge of the range, numerous creeks feed much longer rivers, which meander in a much more tortuous fashion before they too reach the sea.

The high rainfall and the deep friable soils provide an environment that has produced some of the densest temperate eucalypt forests and rainforests in southern Australia. The first explorers of this region were met with forests of unbelievable size and density. Mountain Ash, the world's tallest hardwood, soared to heights of up to 100 metres and dominated an understorey of Musk Daisy Bush, Hazel Pomaderris and a great variety of ferns. In places where fire had occurred, masses of twining grass blocked their way. The many gullies that dissect the range were often deep and inaccessible, and were frequently clothed in rainforest and dominated by ancient Myrtle Beeches.

The geological history of the Otways can be traced back to the early Cretaceous period before Australia split off from Antarctica and drifted northwards during the disintegration of Gondwanaland. The present southern coast is broadly aligned with the ancient rift initiated over 100 million years ago. At that time the area was flat and relatively featureless: a low-lying region of swamps and lakes and meandering streams. Over the millions of years the lakes and depressions filled with sand, silt and mud that was washed off the surrounding hills. An immense period of time elapsed during this process and this is evident from the beds of the sedimentary rock now over 3,000 metres deep. Later, in the Tertiary period which began 60 million years ago, the land subsided, coal beds formed in swamps, and in places the sea breached the low-lying landmass and marine sediments were laid down.

Within the last few million years, the region has been subject to uplifting and faulting, which created the Otways as we know them today. The soft younger Tertiary capping was gradually stripped from the mountains by erosion to reveal the older Cretaceous sediments. Thus, fossilised remains

OPPOSITE: A rainbow forms over Moonlight Head.

1

of ferns and mosses, the original inhabitants of the flat marshy environment, can now be found in places on top of the range.

Volcanic activity occurred in a few isolated places in the region as early as 30 million years ago and is revealed where small basalt flows have been exposed along the coast. Immediately to the north, volcanic activity on a massive scale began much later and ceased only within the last 5,000 years to form the vast volcanic plain along the northern margins of the range.

The Otways are flanked by one of the world's most turbulent seas – Bass Strait. It is this confluence of mountain, dense forest and wild ocean that gives the region its character and that has helped to fashion its history. Biologically the Otways can be thought of as an island. They have been separated from similar forested mountains to the east for over a million years by the basalt lava plain, which coincides with a belt of lower rainfall and supports open grassland rather than forest. They have also been isolated from comparable country in Tasmania by the flooding of Bass Strait following the last Ice Age. So it is not surprising that the Otways exhibit some unusual differences in plant, animal and insect life.

In total I spent 90 days studying this extraordinarily diverse area. Unfortunately I did not have the time to stay for extended periods. On the contrary, most of my observations and photographs came from day trips. Often I left before dawn and returned in the dark. Sometimes I stayed overnight and camped out; occasionally I visited the region with friends, but mostly I was alone. The diaries I kept during this time cover more than two years but in order to emphasise the seasonal changes, I have grouped my visits in the month that they occurred, regardless of the year.

In such an extensive and diverse region, it is important to attempt to examine each major land form. In practice this is difficult to do. I kept revisiting my chosen spots and they were, I think, reasonably representative. It is surprising what variations you find in the same setting over a period of time; as well as the seasonal changes, there are the emerging flowers,

A stormy sky over Lavers Hill.

Tall Mountain Ash
(Eucalyptus regnans*).

insects and fungi and, from a photographic point of view, the light varies constantly.

After each of my visits I followed up my on-the-spot observations with reading and research, although knowledge is advancing so quickly in some areas that ideas and concepts may have changed after publication. The end product is a book speckled randomly with unrelated notes on items of history, natural history, agriculture and conservation, but it reflects the casual and unpredictable way in which an observer sees things and how thoughts and ideas spring to mind.

At the end of the project I felt somewhat frustrated. How can you capture the mood and essence of such a varied landscape? It seems to me that a lifetime could be spent in the Otways seeking those rare moments when a photograph or an observation can say so much so simply. Nevertheless, I hope I have been able to convey some of my own feelings for this unique part of the Australian coastline.

JANUARY

LEFT: A vivid sunrise at Demons Bluff.

ABOVE: An ancient turban shell
(Turbo undulatus) on an
Aboriginal midden.

10 JANUARY

It was pitch-black when I left home at five this morning. My plan was to cover a wide sweep of the Otways from Point Addis, following the Ocean Road, through to Lavers Hill, returning to Melbourne via Gellibrand and Colac. I felt that this would cover a variety of landscapes, including the coast and the mountains, and would provide a cross section of vegetation, ranging from heathland to forest to rainforest.

At Point Addis I took a steep walking track a kilometre northeast of the Point, which leads eastward to the head of the bay. Here the cliffs reach their highest elevation, some 100 metres above the sea. It was still dark as I picked my way cautiously along a narrow track cut between stunted Messmates and Brown Stringybarks. At any time the view from this vantage point is stunning with the cliffs falling away sheer beneath your feet. This morning it was exceptional. It was one of the most vivid sunrises I have experienced. The low sea cloud dispersed the first rays of the sun as they came above the horizon, creating a pink glow which lit up the bay and turned the massive cliffs a bright shade of red.

These towering cliffs, which stretch for 10 kilometres southwest to Anglesea and northeast to beyond Bells Beach and Torquay, never fail to impress me. Cut so cleanly, they have an almost unnatural look save for those sections where rock and soil have slumped, carrying trees and other vegetation which have re-established in precarious positions far below.

The oldest beds in this bluff of sedimentary rocks were laid down at the beginning of the Tertiary period, 60 million years ago. At first, gradual subsidence occurred, leading to the formation of swamps and lakes. Then

Sunrise, Point Addis.

soil and sand eroded from the surrounding hills were deposited to form beds of sandstone. Much later, in the Miocene epoch 26 million years ago, the lowest level of land depression was reached and sea water entered the system of lakes and swamps. Fossils tell this story, changing down the profile from sea-water to freshwater species.

Later this morning at Lorne I braved the rain squalls to examine the rock platform just south of Loutit Bay. The bay takes its name from Captain Loutitt who, in his schooner the *Apollo*, serviced the first two points of European human habitation along this coast in the 1850s and is said to have taken the first boatload of wool from Geelong to London.

The rock platforms are made of smooth grey-green rocks of Cretaceous origin. They contrast sharply with the ochres and yellows of the younger Tertiary sediments that form the cliffs at Anglesea and Point Addis, only a few kilometres to the northeast. The sea was running strongly today. I watched enthralled as huge waves surged past the point into Loutit Bay, the strong offshore wind catching the crests and flinging spray backwards like trailing headdresses.

The late Edmund Gill, a noted scientist, has written graphically of a great storm that raged on 16 and 17 May 1975. Despite popular belief at the time that the storm that created the huge waves was local in origin, the giant swell was the result of a storm thousands of kilometres away in the world's most turbulent sea, the Great Southern Ocean. The local wind in fact blew in the opposite direction, over the Otway Ranges from the northwest.

Having previously surveyed the area of a huge shore platform (212 metres by 57 metres) known locally as Jump Rock, Gill was able to calculate the weight of water which struck and spilled over it. The waves broke on average three times every minute, travelling at 20 kilometres per hour, and an incredible 12,000 tonnes of water struck the platform with each wave. Rocks of up to one and a half tonnes in weight were gouged out of the platform and hurled to the rear against the cliffs. With the sand churned up by the waves, the abrasive action was so great that, by the end of the storm, the rock platforms were polished clean of barnacles, sea snails and other encrustations.

Shore platforms are a major feature of the Otway coastline. They have their origin in the great swells arising in the Southern Ocean. The relatively small tidal range experienced on the coast ensures that the abrading action of the sand picked up by the waves is focused on a narrow band of rock. Because the sandstone is relatively hard, it has resisted the natural ramp-forming action of waves which occurs when they meet sand or soft rock. The waves breaking on the flat shore platform spill out over the surface, the water eventually finding its way to channels in softer parts of the rock or in joints or faults which have widened and deepened over time. Although the platforms appear flat, immediately below the cliff face they have a

The Great Ocean Road.

slightly convex profile, so water is directed back to the channels cut at right angles to the direction of the oncoming waves. Not only do these channels provide the paths through which broken waves can return to the sea, they also receive and recycle waves which enter them directly. Thus the water within the channels is extraordinarily turbulent and well supplied with oxygen, and has a very diverse and specific population of marine creatures, including fish, seaweed and molluscs.

Later, travelling the most winding and precipitous section of the Great Ocean Road between Lorne and Apollo Bay, I was impressed by the engineering skill and dedication which went into its construction over 60 years ago. The idea of a coastal road from Anglesea to Warrnambool originated before the First World War. It was very much the brainchild of the Honourable Howard Hitchock, a Geelong politician and entrepreneur. Hitchock had the vision of a scenic road that would rival South Africa's famous coastal road near Cape Town and would encourage tourism and commercial development. Hitchock also had the drive and energy to make it happen.

The project finally got under way after the war ended and was dedicated as a monument to those who had lost their lives in the conflict. It also provided employment for many returned servicemen who were unable to find work in the early 1920s.

Because of its extremely rugged nature, the coastline would have remained largely unknown to the public were it not for construction of the Great Ocean Road. Given the lack of sophisticated machinery, the huge rocky cliffs and heavily forested sections, and the desire of the planners to have the road follow the coast wherever possible, it was something of an engineering masterpiece. Today it continues to provide access to some of the finest coastal scenery in Australia.

Apollo Bay, first known as Middleton and later by the name of Krambruk, was an important dairy farming district but is now noted as a tourist destination. It was originally developed, however, as a supply of timber. Giant logs of blue gum and Mountain Ash were loaded onto boats at Mounts Bay and transported to Melbourne. This was sometimes a very difficult and hazardous task because of the open nature of the bay and its vulnerability to storms driven by easterly winds. Eventually the timber was cut out and the best of the hills, the valleys and coastal plains were converted to pasture in a land-settlement program begun in the 1870s. Unfortunately, much of the steeper country inland from Apollo Bay proved too hard to manage for farmers and the pasture disappeared under bracken fern, Dogwood and regrowth Blackwood.

A few kilometres beyond Apollo Bay, the Ocean Road swings west and enters much taller and heavier forest country. At first the dominant tree is blue gum. This is the so-called Southern, or Tasmanian Blue Gum (*Eucalyptus globulus*), a tree that provided the earliest source of timber at Apollo Bay where it dominated the original coastal forests. Because of its close similarity to the well-known Tasmanian tree, it was believed by some that the local plants had arisen from seed blown across Bass Strait. The blue gum of Apollo Bay was regarded as of the finest quality as it was exceedingly dense and hard in the grain. The timber was widely used for railway sleepers, for building construction and for shoring up mine shafts. The area, in fact, was a major source of the sleepers used to build the Melbourne to Geelong railway line and the line from Geelong to Ballarat. Another subspecies of blue gum, *Eucalyptus pseudoglobulus*, occurs further inland but did not attract the same interest from sawmillers.

Mountain Ash forest, which succeeds blue gum as you move inland, is sometimes confused with rainforest because the two frequently occur together. The former is classed botanically as wet sclerophyll forest and although it may be growing in the same rainfall belt and on the same soil type, it does not have a closed canopy, nor does it support the same range

Mountain Ash (Eucalyptus regnans).

of ferns and mosses in the understorey. The relationship between these two high rainfall forest types is far from static, the balance being greatly influenced by fire, which encourages the proliferation of Mountain Ash. Although a very hot fire kills mature ash trees, it also promotes regeneration, and in time the new trees encroach on the neighbouring rainforest which is less able to recover from fire. On the other hand, in the absence of wildfires, rainforest gradually invades and replaces the uniform stands of Mountain Ash as the trees age and become less vigorous. A secondary rainforest is then formed comprising Myrtle Beech with a scattering of Mountain Ash and occasional other tall forest trees such as Manna Gum and Southern Blue Gum.

Although the original Mountain Ash and blue gum forests of the Otways have been decimated beyond recognition by milling, agriculture and fire, the area of rainforest has probably not been greatly reduced since settlement. Today nearly 5,000 hectares remain. The reason is partly that Myrtle Beech was never considered an important commercial timber in Victoria, certainly when compared with Mountain Ash, blue gum or Blackwood.

Among the ferns along the creek the most obvious and striking were the very tall and graceful Slender Tree Ferns (*Cyathea cunninghamii*). This species is among the tallest tree ferns in the world and specimens over 20 metres high have been recorded. By growing to this height, these ferns are presumably able to tap into an environment between the overhead canopy and the underlying ferns which experiences different conditions of shade, temperature, wind and humidity.

Travelling on past Maites Rest and covering perhaps another 10 kilometres of heavy forest, the Great Ocean Road comes suddenly to the Calder River

*OPPOSITE: Rainforest dominated by Myrtle Beech (*Nothofagus cunninghamii*).*

BELOW: Verdant pasture near Glenaire.

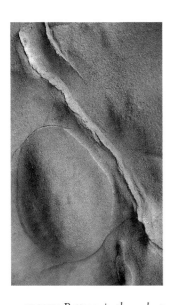

ABOVE: *Patterns in the rock at Castle Cove.*

BELOW: *Silver Gulls.*

and a wide expanse of rich, flat pastureland, originally a swamp on the flood plain of the Aire River. Judging by the sleek appearance of the cattle and the healthy green growth of the pasture, the selection of this land for clearing last century has proved a successful choice. But were it not for the line of fortuitously located sand dunes separating pastures from the ocean, this would be a very bleak area indeed. Without the dunes it would receive the full force of the southwest gales which blow in almost continuously from Bass Strait.

This tranquil rural scene ends abruptly a few kilometres further on at Glenaire where the road rises steeply and skirts the dunes, giving the first full view of the turbulent waters of Bass Strait. This was an opportunity for me to explore the beach, some 50 metres below. The cliffs are interestingly coloured – an assortment of the grey-green sandstone I saw earlier along the east coast, but here mixed with layers of lighter coloured mudstones. These rocks are softer than the sandstones and have mostly disappeared from the shore platforms east of Cape Otway; but because here they are at higher levels in the cliff face, they remain protected from the abrading action of the waves.

My final point of call today was Melba Gully. Now declared a State park, this has long been recognised as one of the most beautiful fern gullies in the Otways. It was named after Dame Nellie Melba by a Mrs Fry, who purchased the property in 1921. Surprisingly, given the seemingly pristine nature of this enchanting glade, it and the neighbouring Lavers Gully were once the sites of sawmilling operations. The first mill was established by Charley Robins in about 1916 close to the present park headquarters. Later, William Angliss & Company erected another mill next to the Crowes Railway Station, 500 metres uphill to the north on the narrow-gauge railway line to Colac. This latter sawmill was specially equipped to produce staves for the tallow barrels used at Angliss's huge Melbourne meat works.

The small steep valley of the Johanna River which drops from here 500 metres to the sea in only 15 kilometres is encompassed by the park and dominated by ancient Myrtle Beeches. In sunlight the beeches cast a dark yet dappled shadow over all things beneath them. Nothing the camera can record captures the magic of this scene. In a technical sense, on a sunny day the range of light values is just too great to record on film. By unconscious selection, the human eye is able to view the full beauty of the scene whereas, in my experience, the camera invariably produces a disappointing result,

no matter whether you expose on the highlights, the lowlights or somewhere
in between. On a dull day the results are likely to be better because the
range of light values is not so extreme, but sometimes the long exposures
needed lead to colour distortion. These scenes are quite the most frustrating
I have tried to capture on film.

Above the rapids on the Johanna River the track leads up steeply by
way of cut steps to a tree of huge proportions, though unfortunately it
is in a fairly advanced state of decay, having survived numerous fires and
wind storms. It has been officially measured at 37 metres around the base
but it is now no longer anywhere near its original height. The top branches
have broken away and much of the tree appears to be dead. It is an example
of the Otway Messmate, a hybrid of the Mountain Ash and the Messmate.
Hybridisation among eucalypts of different species is common enough because

many species are genetically very similar. Where related species occur close together, hybrid or intermediate populations are sometimes found.

The final section of the Melba Gully walk leads through less luxuriant vegetation on a ridge, finally winding down through a fern gully. Here I found some beautiful moss displays on the bank next to the pathway; particularly striking was the spreading and procumbent foliage of Dog's Tooth Moss. Some of these mosses look superficially like tiny ferns. They are very ancient plants like ferns but even more primitive. They have no flowers and the sexual organs, the antheridia and archegonia, are located separately on the ends of the stems and are often easily visible. Following fertilisation a spore-bearing capsule develops and after germination each germinating spore produces a threadlike organ called a protonema. New moss plants develop from buds on the protonema.

15 JANUARY

TOP: Orb-weaving spider (Eriophora sp).

BOTTOM: Female orb-weaving spider (Eriophora pustulosa) photographed on its web at night.

The Bellarine Peninsula was shrouded in a dense haze which obscured the view on either side of the road. I wondered whether the haze was a sea mist or from a bushfire, or whether it was coming from the smoke stack of the brown-coal (lignite) generating plant. No fire was reported in the area yesterday.

I spent the day wandering the woodlands bordering the cliffs, a few kilometres northeast of the Anglesea township. Classed botanically as heathy woodland, it is the most extensive of several kinds of vegetation in the Anglesea district. The principal trees are Messmate and Brown Stringybark. They form an open canopy and are widely separated, allowing sunlight to penetrate freely and to encourage the mass of smaller plants in the understorey.

The Anglesea Heath has the richest flora in Victoria and one of the most diverse in the world. Apart from rainforests, it is believed to be only exceeded in plant variety by some heathlands in Western Australia and in the Cape Province of South Africa. No less than 162 species have been recorded in a single hectare of heathy woodland at Anglesea.

A Christmas Spider or Six-spined Spider had spun a web across the path I was following. I was able to photograph it, but it was difficult to retain in focus because it proved so active. Christmas Spiders have an extraordinarily spiny appearance. They are usually black in colour with yellow and white markings on the abdomen. This particular specimen was a female. The abdomen, one centimetre or so in diameter, is considerably larger than that of the male, which is otherwise similar in appearance. The spiders mate during the summer months and the females then lay their eggs, with young spiderlings emerging during the succeeding winter.

Christmas Spiders are one of a group of orb-weaving spiders that construct their webs with a central sticky spiral thread into which their hapless insect victims fly. Sometimes they occur in huge colonies covering large areas of bushland. Their individual webs become so enmeshed that it is difficult to determine who owns what. I recall once attempting to photograph a flowering bladderwort in a swamp and having to brave a solid phalanx of webs and crawling spiders to reach my camera subject.

While I was photographing, a flock of Red Wattlebirds joined me briefly, settling on a stunted Messmate. Shortly afterwards, they made off noisily. Long before you see these birds you can readily identify them by their

LEFT: *A Christmas or Six-spined Spider* (Gasteracantha minax).

ABOVE: *A hovering fly (Bombyliidae) suspended by fast-moving wings above a flower of the Prickly Tea Tree* (Leptospermum juniperinum).

harsh and raucous cries. Wattlebirds are much bigger and less elegant than other Australian honeyeaters. They are much the largest species you see around here. The flower of the Silver Banksia is a favourite source of nectar for them, though this is more often an autumn and winter flowering plant at Anglesea. There are no other obvious flowering plants to attract them on the heathland at the present time. However, like many other honeyeaters, they are also insectivorous and it's quite possible they were looking for insects today.

I found and photographed some large orb-weaving spiders, interestingly patterned in brown and white with white-banded legs. This particular spider, when disturbed, coils up and falls to the ground, feigning death. In this position they are difficult to see among the twigs and leaves on the ground. Another spider, a leaf-dwelling species, was very active in restoring its web as the wind, which had just sprung up, made havoc with it. The spider leapt out from its cylindrical shelter in the centre of the web, climbing on a single invisible strand to a neighbouring leaf, seemingly to effect repairs, then raced back to its lair.

I was intrigued to watch a hoverfly suspended motionless in the air. It would hold its position for a few seconds then suddenly dart at lightning speed to another spot and again remain seemingly suspended.

I noted a large longhorn grasshopper on a flowering tea tree. It was boldly patterned in green and white and yet surprisingly difficult to see as it sat quite motionless on the leaves.

At 2.15 pm, the weather changed suddenly as the sea mist rolled in, light rain began falling and the temperature dropped noticeably. The heathland took on an almost wintry look. I took some photographs from a big hill above the Laterite Peak looking westerly towards the Angahook Reserve. It was a grim and stormy scene.

21 JANUARY

At Point Roadknight, near Anglesea, huge masses of seaweed had been washed up on the sheltered bay-side of the point. They were piled up to a depth of 70 centimetres, covering the shoreline rocks and making progress along the foreshore quite hazardous. The slimy seaweed beneath my feet caused me to slide suddenly and unexpectedly off concealed rocks. There were at least 10 species of seaweed that I could see with my unskilled eye and a great range of colour and form.

Tiny grey-white crustaceans scampered everywhere. These creatures live on washed-up seaweed and play an important part in its breakdown. Clearly there must have been a powerful storm in recent days to remove such

TOP: *Enlarged pedicel and fruit of Wild Cherry* (Exocarpos cupressiformis).

RIGHT: *Accumulations of seaweed* (Eklonia radiata).

BOTTOM: *A red seaweed* (Plocamium *sp*).

large quantities from the seafloor. Such huge losses seem to occur quite frequently. The constant cycle of destruction and regeneration must be important in providing nutrients for both the marine and intertidal inhabitants. I photographed a small pink fernlike seaweed which included strange shell-like plates. Some red seaweeds (Corallines) often accumulate lime and bleach white and become brittle when they dry out on the beach after being washed in.

Inland on a Wild Cherry tree, I located some pupae of the Wood White butterfly. A number had already emerged but one was due to come out soon, and the wing colours were visible through the pupae case. This butterfly, like other members of the Jezebel or Delias group, feeds on mistletoe; but unlike them will also feed on the parasitic tree, Wild Cherry, a relative of mistletoe that attaches itself to tree roots rather than branches.

The Wild Cherries had a few fruits on them: strange small red and green objects with red coloured pedicels – the original flower stalks – much larger than the fruit. One interesting variation I found had a purplish receptacle and a yellow fruit. They were about the size of a fat peanut and tasted quite sweet with a light yet subtle flavour. Wild Cherry fruits were a part of the diet of Aborigines.

Later this afternoon on the heathland I found a small cicada still soft and unable to fly following emergence from the nymphal shell. There are a great number of species of these small cicadas but they are often hard to find and can usually only be located by means of the piercing sound they make. In practice this is very difficult to do, and few people seem able to locate exactly the source of the sound.

The cicadas' song appears to be designed primarily to attract the attention of fellow male cicadas (only the males produce sound) as well as females. The males tend to congregate in small areas and the combined sound from dozens of cicadas in a single tree or a small copse of bushland on a hot summer's day is quite deafening. It is also believed that the piercing sound of a cicada choir may act as a deterrent to marauding birds.

Such is the sensitivity of communication between a group of singing cicadas that the song seems to start or end in a split second as though at the command of a hidden conductor. This popular belief, however, has been challenged by entomologists who claim that a leader among the cicadas makes the initial move with the others following within a few seconds.

Recently emerged cicada
(Diemeniana euronotiana).

Condemned to a subterranean life of total darkness and feeding on tree roots, the nymph lives several years as a soft, white, wingless creature, whose well-developed compound eyes are actually covered by an opaque layer, presumably to protect them as it burrows in search of food. The exact lifespan of most cicada species is not known, but one well-documented American species spends 17 years below the ground in preparation for a joyous few days of sun and song!

Tongue orchids, which favour swampy sites, have made an appearance on the low-lying section of heathland. But even here moisture may have been limiting because only one specimen had managed to flower. Tongue orchids belong to the genus *Crypostylis* with five species occurring in Australia. They have a strange flower with a labellum that looks quite like a tongue with a pink and red undersurface and which curls upwards as the flower opens. The bizarre appearance of tongue orchids is enhanced by the fact that the flower is borne upside down on the plant with the labellum (normally a somewhat drooping floral part of an orchid) inclining upward.

They emit a scent which is apparently identical to the sex attractant (pheromones) of a large blue and red wasp (*Lissopimpla excelsa*) which attempts to mate with the flower. In so doing, it collects the sticky pollinia (the pollen-containing organs) and when it visits the next tongue orchid flower some pollen may be transferred to the female portion of the flower, thus achieving cross-pollination. Certainly the adaptations of orchids to achieve

cross-pollination (out-crossing) by means of a variety of insect vectors are among the most striking examples in nature of the coevolution of quite unrelated organisms. But the tongue orchid's strategy of having a wasp mate with its flower must surely be one of the most extraordinary.

This afternoon I discovered a colony of the Bright Copper butterfly feeding on Sweet Bursaria growing along Salt Creek, which meanders through the Anglesea heath. This was an exciting discovery. Mary White, a local naturalist, had originally noted the species from the lookout close to Anglesea township, but it appears that the colony was destroyed by the very severe 1983 Ash Wednesday fire and she has not seen them since.

This patch of bushland along Salt Creek was burnt in an earlier and less devastating fire in 1980. Although the Bright Copper would seem particularly vulnerable to fire because it usually occurs in discrete colonies, it is possible that only a very severe fire which burns right into the ground, like that of Ash Wednesday, would actually destroy the sheltering caterpillars. They live at the base of the Sweet Bursaria plant where they are attended by small black ants. They cling to the trunk and the roots below the ground during daylight, emerging at night to forage on leaves. During a fire, I imagine, the larvae would retreat several centimetres below the surface as the soil heated up, and would thus be protected. They have considerable capacity to go without food and may be able to survive long enough for the foliage to reshoot after fire. Larvae of the family of blue butterflies (Lycaenidae) to which these Coppers belong are notorious for being cannibalistic. In captivity large ones will readily eat smaller ones of their brethren. Could this be a survival mechanism for the these seemingly vulnerable insects in their widely separated colonies? It would take some weeks for the food plant to shoot again and the few cannibal larvae who had completed their life cycle would ensure the colony's survival.

ABOVE LEFT: The moment of truth as a cicada (Cyclochila australasiae) emerges from its nymphal shell after several years underground in total darkness.

ABOVE: Male Bright Copper butterfly (Paralucia aurifer).

23&24 JANUARY

The Western District beyond Geelong has dried out a good deal since my last visit. The roadside clumps of Phalaris stand out with their neat, pale green, flowering heads a metre or more above the ground. Paddock feed, now dry, it still abundant here. It is a treeless, lonely landscape. There are few remnant paddock trees, mostly red gums with some cypresses and

pines around the farmhouses and occasional formal plantations of Sugar Gums. In one paddock, a number of River Red Gums still survive, as do the dead skeletons of others, the latter twisted into a variety of weird and tortured shapes almost always bent in the direction of the prevailing westerly wind. I wondered just how much more tree cover there was at the time of European settlement. It seems that there were more trees then but it was always an open parklike landscape and this undoubtedly added to its attraction to the newly arrived pastoralists. Native and introduced grasses grew vigorously on the basalt soils, the flat landscape made for ease of movement of both stock and vehicles, and a minimum of clearing was required.

The early settlers were not without their thinkers and visionaries, men who saw the aesthetic value of trees and their importance in the maintenance of soil and shelter for stock. Some became concerned at the rate of disappearance of native vegetation and began actively to plant trees. Foremost amongst these innovators was JL Currie who grew his first plantation on his station, Larra, near Darlington in 1851. He later developed a method of distributing eucalypt seed on newly ploughed land. At the time of his death in 1889, Currie had over 1,700 acres of plantations on his extensive holdings. He was not alone and other prominent pastoralist families, including the Armytages of Woolomatta at Lara and their neighbours, the Fairbairns and the Chirnesides at Glencoe in South Australia, also grew extensive belts of plantation trees or fenced off and protected native vegetation. It was Currie, however, who not only initiated this early green movement but who also identified the outstanding suitability of the Sugar Gum for the environment of the volcanic plains. His experiments showed this seemingly unlikely species from the much drier climate of the Eyre Peninsula of South Australia to be superior to all other types of trees that had been tried. Currie's legacy is seen today in the plantations of these tall straight trees that line fences, laneways and roads throughout the Western District.

I took the road south from Winchelsea to Deans Marsh. Here the pastures are considerably greener and clearly this district has received some summer rain. All along the roadside here at this time of the year are masses of yellow firewood (*Senecio linearifolius*). Although its popular name suggests it is a weed, this is not strictly true. It is a native species which occupies clearings caused as a result of timber removal or through the actions of fire. It does not seem to spread beyond its natural habitat.

Throughout the forest there is still much evidence of previous milling. Many old stumps still bear the deep cuts which supported the planks on which the axemen stood as they cut down the trees. Crosscut saws were also used to cut the logs. The logs were then hauled by means of wire ropes on a steam-powered winch to a landing alongside the tramway leading to the sawmill. Winch lines were half a kilometre or more in length. Where timber extraction had been in progress for some time, it was often necessary to use a jinker team of horses to pull the logs to the end of the winch line, known as the head block. Logs were usually accompanied by two men: a rope man who guided the chocker (the attaching rope around the log) and the rope-whistle man. The latter signalled instructions to the winch operator back at the landing by means of tugs on the whistle rope. Five whistle signals were used; one meant stop, two – go ahead, three – come back, four – slack off, and five indicated there had been an accident. On reaching the landing, logs were rolled onto the trucks powered in the early days by teams of horses and later by small steam-powered locomotives, and hauled to the sawmills.

I returned later in the afternoon to the Ocean Road and made my way down to Moonlight Beach, about 15 kilometres southwest of Lavers Hill. The beach takes its name from Moonlight Head, a prominence to the east, first seen by Matthew Flinders on a stormy evening on his voyage through Bass Strait in 1803. In his diary he briefly noted the silhouette of the high cliffs as was revealed by the light of the moon as it emerged momentarily from behind clouds.

I hoped for some late-afternoon photographs. The tide was well out and gave an opportunity for some unusual shots. On the beach nearby, I photographed seaweed ranging in colour from mauve to white piled up in lines left by the retreating waves. The pods or floats of certain species of seaweed were very noticeable, along with a good deal of flotsam and jetsam, much of it unfortunately made up of coloured plastic bottles.

The next day, after a rainy night at Lavers Hill, I noted how everywhere

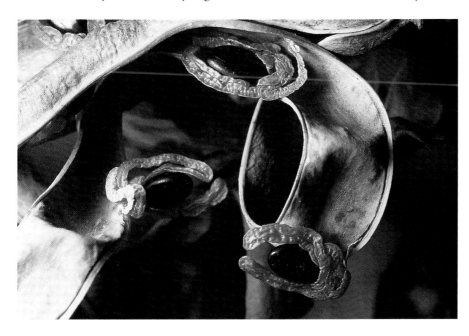

Seeds and seed pod of Blackwood (Acacia melanoxylon).

ABOVE: Flowers of Ragwort (Senecio jacobaea).

RIGHT: Lichens (Baeomyces sp), Turtons Track.

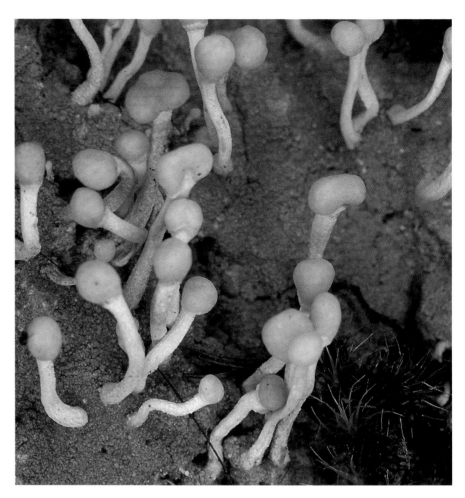

along the Beach Forest Road seedlings of Blackwood were coming up, almost to the exclusion of all else. There must be a great bank of Blackwood seed in the soil, possibly dating back to late last century when the Otway Ridge was cleared of its dense forest cover for farmland. The Blackwood seed has a very hard coat and can exist in the ground for many years, germinating only after a hot fire that burns into the humus layer below the soil.

The weed Ragwort can be seen here and there in the paddocks near Lavers Hill. It was evident that plants have recently been pulled out with some left along the side of the road. This weed, more than any other, has been the scourge of farmers in the elevated regions of the Otways and the Gippsland hills. Of European origin, Ragwort is thought to have entered Victoria in chaff from New Zealand fed to horses working in southern Gippsland timber mills in the early nineteen hundreds.

The great natural difficulty of clearing and farming these areas was accentuated during the First World War when many farmers joined the armed forces. Many farms were left untended and Ragwort gradually gained a hold, often to the exclusion of other useful plant species. The seed of Ragwort does not spread far from the parent plant, although it can be windborne by means of small, hairy 'parachutes' attached to the seed. It is extraordinarily prolific – a single plant produces as many as 250,000 seeds in one year.

The control of Ragwort in pastures relies on cultivation to bury seed and roots to a depth which prevents regrowth. It also depends on the use of chemical sprays and the employment of crossbred sheep to eat the plant and prevent its flowering. Sheep, unlike cattle and horses, are not much affected by a poisonous alkaloid called jacobine that is contained in Ragwort. In the last 20 years, the return of much of the badly-infected areas to Mountain

Ash and pine plantations has reduced the problem. However, it still remains a major concern on farmland and continues to spread into clean properties in the foothills.

Biological control would seem a logical method, and a number of other weeds have been controlled by this means. Biological control depends on the introduction of insects or fungi which prey on the particular weed in its country or district of origin. With Ragwort, however, this tactic has not so far proved a success. The brightly coloured red and purple Cinnabar moth imported from Europe many years ago failed to establish because of attacks on it by local fungi and bacteria and also from the effects of desiccation in our drier climate. Another natural enemy of the weed, the Ragwort Seed Fly also made no impression when introduced. A couple of native moth species will attack Ragwort from time to time, but exert no significant control over it.

There is some wonderful forest scenery along Turtons Track which links the towns of Beech Forest and Apollo Bay. There are few other places I know where it is possible to obtain such uninterrupted views of the towering, slender, white-trunked Mountain Ash. These soaring trees make a wonderful contrast to the mass of dense, richly-green ferns which clothe the creek along the winding road and also with the darker green Myrtle Beech.

The plants of Christmas Bush at Turtons Track are huge and today were covered in cascades of white flowers. I photographed two flowers close-up; they seem often to be borne in pairs on a small inflorescence. I noticed that the flowers here appear somewhat paler than those found in eastern Victoria. However, they have that same beautiful, purplish colour in the throat below where the petals join. Although growing much taller than its relatives, the Christmas Bush is one of the mint bushes and when I crushed the leaves a very powerful mintlike odour was quickly evident.

I left Turtons Track at midday to have a look at the Beauchamp Falls and it was well worth the visit. The falls picnic area is set in a grove of Douglas Fir planted many years ago. They were planted in the 1930s on abandoned farmlands and adjacent forests. The timber, oregon, is much prized and has been imported from northwest United States and Canada to build homes in this country for over a century. The timber from the Otway trees is generally good, though the core is often soft so that larger and older trees have to be selected. However, Douglas Fir has not become a dominant plantation timber here because it takes too long to mature – 60 years or more compared to the 35 years for Radiata Pine. The closely growing rows provide a very dense canopy and with the consequent dim light there is virtually no growth beneath them.

Flowers of Christmas Bush
(Prostanthera lasianthos).

FEBRUARY

LEFT: A summer pastoral patchwork, Weeaproinah.

ABOVE: Seedling Mountain Ash (Eucalyptus regnans), Lavers Hill.

4 & 5 FEBRUARY

The pastures are well and truly dried out now. But there is a good body of standing feed in the paddocks of the Western District between Geelong and Colac. This is surprising given the very poor early spring when paddocks as late as October looked more like winter pastures with short yellowish grass; but the extraordinarily late spring rains changed all that. Fortunately, the cool weather has also ensured an uneventful bushfire season so far, although there would be much to burn were we now to get an extended hot and dry spell. Hopefully it is too late in the season for that to happen.

My plan for the trip was to look first at the Gellibrand district which, like much of the other country on the Tertiary sediments, is dominated by Messmate and Shining Peppermint. It seemed to me a good locality to look for insects, particularly if I could locate some Sweet Bursaria. I recall reading an article written by an entomologist, FE Wilson, in the 1920s in which he recorded several interesting insects at Gellibrand in January, including the beautiful red and black jewel beetle, *Stigmodera bremei*. When Sweet Bursaria is in flower, it is a magnet for insects, although its attractiveness varies greatly with its maturity. The problem is that the Bursaria here seems to favour the heavier soils, and most of this country is very light – the heavier country has been cleared and is now in pasture. As a result, I found it very difficult to locate any plants. I did, however, find a patch in a roadside reserve and, although it was not particularly attractive to insects, there were a few butterflies, beetles and flies on the clumps of small cream-white flowers. The flowers have a very pungent sweet smell, which presumably lures the insects to them.

On the Bursaria I found an assassin bug, resplendent in black and orange, belonging to the family Reduviidae, which had transfixed a small fly with its curved beak. The assassin bug injects a narcotising fluid which renders its prey unconscious, and then proceeds to suck out the body fluids. This particular species is common on Bursaria flowers, where it lurks to catch unwary insects. These bugs are generally accepted to be beneficial insects in that they prey on insect pests, but some species can inflict a painful bite if you handle them carelessly.

*A reduvid bug (*Gminatus australis*) and captured fly (unidentified) on Sweet Bursaria (*Bursaria spinosa*).*

*Jewel beetle (*Castiarina bremei *formerly* Stigmodera bremei*) was commonly found around Gellibrand many years ago.*

Seeking more suitable country for Bursaria, I took the road from Gellibrand up onto the Otway Ridge. The few places I looked along the roadside were covered with dust from the dirt road raised by passing traffic and thus were bereft of any insect visitors, although the flowers were plentiful.

Where the road enters the forest country at the foot of the ranges there were some excellent stands of what I took to be Manna Gum. These had beautiful trunk colours, and much loose bark hanging from the lower limbs. I also located and photographed a Slender Tree Fern.

I camped the night among the she-oaks above Moonlight Beach and listened to the sighing of these trees in the strong southerly wind until I fell asleep. I had hoped to attract insects – particularly moths – to my gas lamp, but it was apparently too cold and nothing came in. I did note, however, a small pink moth on a leaf of a grass tree. This particular specimen settled

ABOVE: *Reflections in a pool on Loves Creek, Gellibrand.*

ABOVE RIGHT: *Moth (Heliocausta sp, family Oecophoridae).*

with its wings tightly closed and flatly pressed along the line of the grass tree leaf. I think it is a member of the family Oecophoridae, which is extremely well represented in Australia, and contains many small but beautifully marked and coloured species.

There are no less than 2,300 species of these moths that have been identified in Australia and many feed on what seems the ultimate in a poor diet – dead leaves. Eucalyptus leaves are a major food source and the dry conditions found over much of the Australian continent guarantee that the tough leaves of these trees will disintegrate very slowly. The Oecophoridae appear to have evolved alongside the genus *Eucalyptus*, enabling them to exploit a food source neglected by other insects.

The next day I was determined to get some very early morning shots of a boulder beach at Ryan Den a few kilometres to the east of Moonlight Beach. When I left at four-thirty there was a clear sky and new moon, and on my way I could not resist the opportunity to take a photograph from the Gable, one of Australia's highest sea cliffs, of the moon over Moonlight Head.

At Ryan Den the tide was out and the rock platform to the west exposed. I photographed the boulder beach as the sun rose, the large boulders, draped with an array of seaweeds and wet with the wash from the waves, reflecting the first rays of sunlight.

Boulder beaches are a feature of this section of the Otway coast. Often they occur near the mouth of a stream from which the boulders may have been disgorged over a period of thousands of years. Other accumulations may represent stones that have been gouged out of cliff faces by the giant waves thrown up in the occasional violent storms that lash this coast. The boulders usually occur in small bays where they are presumably first washed in and then trapped, to be ceaselessly caressed and worn smooth by waves. The process is certainly not a recent phenomenon and ancient boulder beds can frequently be found well back from the sea and often covered with many layers of sand and soil.

The boulders here today were marked with splashes of heavy black oil, released recently from a vessel in Bass Strait. Efforts to identify the offending ship have apparently failed. The effects will be felt for many weeks to come and it is rated as one of the worst oil spills ever along this section of coast. Several penguins have been found washed up in the last week or two.

I disturbed a very large flock of perhaps 100 Little Ravens that wheeled above the cliff in the strange swooping flight they have. For many years the Little Raven was thought to be the same species as the Australian Raven. They not only look almost identical, but their distribution in Australia overlaps so that both birds may be seen in the one district at the same time. What separates the two species are their habits. The Little Raven is nomadic, forms large flocks, nests in small trees and forages widely in search of food, whereas the Australian Raven tends to live in discrete territories. Unlike the Australian Raven, the Little Raven, although a meat eater and a scavenger, has a slender bill better adapted for capturing and eating insects which provide a high proportion of its diet.

I located several sea stars, one blue and another light mauve, with interesting darker markings in the centre of the star. The sea star is an extraordinarily varied creature with seemingly dozens of shades, often sombre hues of brown, olive green or grey, but every now and then you are startled to find a bright red one. Still others can be found that are orange, bright green and even blue. Why they should be so variable in colour is difficult

Setting moon, Moonlight Head.

29

to explain and perhaps there is no reason. They have no predators and one explanation that has been advanced to explain their variability is that it may reflect small differences in diet, the pigments perhaps being derived from different molluscs that they eat.

Sea stars do not have the clearly defined 'arms' of starfish. But this particular species (*Patiriella calcar*) is distinguished from its immediate cousins (five species occur in southern Australian waters) because its star shape is much more evident and it has eight arms rather than the usual five.

The sea star is itself a predatory creature and by an extraordinary act of contortion extrudes its stomach through its mouth to envelop and later digest its prey. Sometimes its victims are bivalve shellfish, whose close-fitting shells defy the sharpest of knives and try the most patient of fishermen. Sea stars open bivalves by applying a relatively small force to separate the two valves, but they apply it over such a long period of time that the shellfish's muscles eventually weaken and the shell opens.

OPPOSITE PAGE:

TOP LEFT: Sunrise on a boulder beach at Ryan Den.

TOP RIGHT: The Waratah sea anemone (Actinia tenebrosa).

BOTTOM: Multicoloured sea stars (Patiriella calcar).

BELOW: An Anglesea River sunrise.

12 FEBRUARY

I made a late start today at 1.15 pm for a visit to the Anglesea heathlands. The paddocks are dry now but there is more feed than one would normally see in summer pastures. There are still tinges of green along the creeks and low-lying portions of the fields.

I was struck by just how little is now in bloom on the heathlands. Despite the 600 or so plants that occur here, only a few Common Heath, Bent

ABOVE: *Crested Tern.*

TOP RIGHT: *A grasshopper* (Cirphula pyrrhocnemis) *which blends in perfectly with a background of lichen-covered rock.*

BOTTOM RIGHT: *Grasshopper* (Goniaea australasiae) *whose colour and shape make it difficult to see on dead leaves.*

Goodenia and Tall Lobelia plants were in flower. The one exception was a number of Messmates (*Eucalyptus obliqua*) in full flower with a profusion of creamy-white blossoms and with a strong, sweet perfume.

On one tree I noticed dozens of insects flying around the masses of furry blossoms. There were large red and metallic blue wasps, several kinds of flies, other species of wasps, and numerous kinds of beetles. And yet none of the equally spectacular flowering trees alongside had any insect visitors. The time of flowering and nectar-flow of eucalypts does not always seem to be synchronised and one wonders if a sequential time of flowering and of peak nectar-flow may favour pollination in some way.

During the late afternoon I noticed a few grasshoppers about. They are hard enough in warm conditions to follow in flight and often extremely difficult to locate once they have settled. One specimen I finally crept close enough to to photograph on a piece of rock had markings just like a crustose lichen – green and grey blotches on a grey background. Its background colour not only matched the rock but its markings allowed for the fact that the rock surface was dotted with lichen. A second grasshopper, small and wingless and perhaps still in the nymphal stage of development, alighted on dead eucalyptus leaves against which its colour and outline disappeared. The effectiveness of the cryptic colouration of grasshoppers is certainly impressive, but so equally is their uncanny ability to select just the right object on which to land.

I stayed back until sunset to photograph the contours of the rounded hills. While the sun set there were some interesting cloud patterns as a storm blew up to the west. I had to wait a long time for the few short bursts of fading sunshine which momentarily lit up the rolling heathlands, highlighting the individual eucalypts with their shining new yellow-green leaves. The silhouette of taller timber on the distant ridges against a stormy sky provided a dramatic atmosphere, and old grass trees in the foreground on the summit of the hill where I stood provided a strong point of interest.

15 & 16 FEBRUARY

I saw two Yellow-tailed Black Cockatoos near Simpson today. They flew lazily out of a farmhouse garden. These large and noisy birds seem to have become used to people over the years since settlement and are a good deal less wary than Sulphur-crested Cockatoos. The slow beat of their wings is one of their most characteristic features. They also appear most often in small flocks. I think the greatest number I have seen together down here in recent years is 15, although I recall seeing much larger flocks in western Victoria years ago.

Early morning light on pastures near Weeaproinah.

ABOVE: Karkalla or Pigface
(Carpobrotus rossii), *a native*
plant found on the dunes.

RIGHT: Marram Grass
(Ammophila arenaria).

There is very little of the once very extensive Heytesbury Forest remaining today. It was largely cleared for farming 25 years ago. The odd pockets left look somehow forlorn and will unfortunately deteriorate further unless carefully looked after. I noticed a good deal of regrowth wattle on the roadside. I did not stop to examine it but it looked like Varnish Wattle.

At Gibsons Steps on the coast near Princetown, I was again impressed by the extensive Marram Grass plantings. Marram Grass was first introduced at Port Fairy 50 kilometres west of here in 1883 from seeds supplied from the government botanist, Baron von Mueller. In fact, it was the first southern hemisphere sowing of this grass native to the coastlines of Europe. Marram is a summer growing perennial which spreads by underground stems or rhizomes. It is remarkable for its ability to thrive and multiply on bare sand drifts and to respond even more vigorously when wind-driven sand attempts to smother it.

The seeds supplied by von Mueller to the borough council of Port Fairy were carefully sown and nurtured by a local ranger, ST Avery. Not content to propagate it by runners sown at wide intervals in the dunes as recommended, Avery planted whole pieces of plants in two-metre rows and at half-metre intervals to produce what was called a plantation. He also lined the rows along the dune contours to give maximum protection against the strong prevailing southwesterly winds. The results were spectacular, delighting the council, the ratepayers and particularly the Baron whose original idea it was.

News of Avery's success soon spread and a small export industry sprang up at Port Fairy with plant materials sent to all parts of Australia as well as the United Kingdom, New Zealand, Brazil and South Africa. However, many people found it hard to believe that such a flourishing stand of grass could be so easily grown on bare sand and some were frankly sceptical. On receipt of cuttings delivered from Port Fairy, the engineer at Newcastle cabled back complaining that 'grass arrived totally useless, nothing but straw'. The reply cable urged him 'to plant the cut straw as directed', which he reluctantly did and was later so ecstatic with the result that he presented the Port Fairy town clerk with a gold pencilcase, and Mr Avery with a set of studs!

Marram Grass is not only a more effective dune-stabilising plant than the original native species, but there is also evidence that the foredunes – those dunes nearest the sea – when vegetated by Marram, are taller and steeper than those populated by native plants. Foredunes are created when wind blowing across a beach is slowed by surface obstructions to a speed where the sand it carries can no longer be supported. Small mounds or ridges can be formed over static objects on the beach, such as rocks or logs, but once covered, such mounds are smoothed out by the prevailing winds and cease to grow. However, plants that colonise the windswept saline environment of the back beach, such as Sea Rocket and Sea Wheat Grass, grow through the sand and ensure that the minidune continues to develop. Marram, since it responds best to freshwater, tends to take over as a secondary coloniser and, with its unrivalled capacity to grow through accumulating sand, it accelerates the rate of dune formation.

Marram has a compact tussock habit of growth and, with its vigour in rising above the accumulating sand, encourages steep dune formation. In fact, the leading edge of Marram-clothed dunes may exceed the angle of repose of sand and in time fall away. Less obviously, larger dunes favoured by Marram Grass must inevitably remove more sand from circulation and

Spider webs amid Myrtle Beech (Nothofagus cunninghamii) *and tree ferns.*

FOLLOWING PAGE: *Old relic spars of Mountain Ash* (Eucalyptus regnans) *tell of previous bushfires.*

in time one assumes that this will have consequences on the formation of coastal features such as spits and sandbanks.

I stayed overnight at Lavers Hill and awoke early to take some dawn photographs. The rolling pastureland near Weeaproinah attracted my interest. These are very gentle hills now mostly cleared, with patches of Blackwood in the gullies and a few remnant Mountain Ash, and associated smaller trees such as Hazel Pomaderris and Musk Daisy Bush. Unfortunately for the photographer, the integrity of these early morning landscapes is so often spoiled by the ever-present electricity wires not readily visible to the naked eye but unfortunately always picked up on film.

Some huge ancient spars of Mountain Ash in a relic forest behind a dairy farm provided an interesting backlit scene against the disk of the rising sun. They are old Mountain Ash presumably killed in a fire many years ago and still with 30 metres or so of dead wood rearing up, somehow still stark and proud. In the open paddocks most of these dead trees have now fallen but they do better in the forests surrounded by young, regrowth timber. I wonder how many more years they will continue to stand.

25 & 26 FEBRUARY

I left home this morning at five o'clock. The days are now noticeably shorter and it was very dark at this hour. I reached the junction of the Rotten Point and Dinosaur Cove tracks as the sun was beginning to appear and a cloud layer was breaking up. The walk to Rotten Point is through low growing Messmate, Prickly Tea Tree and patches of open heathland. At the stage where the track begins its sharp descent down the cliffs, however, the vegetation is quickly replaced by lower growing Coast Beard Heath and Daisy Bush.

Rotten Point dominates the eastern end of the very extensive Johanna Beach, which takes its name from a boat wrecked in the 1850s. It first came into general prominence in the late 1960s when the world surfing

RIGHT: Old turban shell (Turbo undulatus) on Aboriginal midden.

OPPOSITE: Rotten Point looking west towards Johanna Beach.

ABOVE: *Wind-blasted roots of old trees.*

BELOW: *A beetle of the family Rhipiceridae.*

championships at Bells Beach had to be abandoned because of the poor weather, and the finals were transferred to Johanna. Today the long lines of surf were beautifully revealed on the very dark blue waters stretching back many kilometres beyond the mouth of the river to Lion Head.

It is easy to envisage how Rotten Point may have gained its name as pieces of rock are constantly falling away down into the surf below; although, strangely, the earlier maps have it as Rotton Point. The point itself is divided into a western and eastern extremity separated by a tiny bay whose steep almost vertical rock walls are continuously pounded by the sea. Everywhere on the western headland are boulders of fantastic shapes and colours, much of the rock being heavily honeycombed to form what is known in geological terms as tefoni, a rock feature usually found close to sea level where the rock is subject to the weathering effects of saltwater spray. The strange colour and shape of these surface rocks are highlighted by the fact that in places they are lying on a rock surface which is strangely smooth, light yellow and even white in colour.

To reach the rocks at Rotten Point I had to negotiate two sand blowouts – huge cup-shape excavations carved out of the overlying sand by the prevailing westerly winds. They are located on a saddle leading to the point. The second and most westerly of these blowouts has, at one stage, been the site of an Aboriginal midden and the eroded surface is covered with old weathered and broken shells. At the northern edge the midden shells are clearly revealed in large layers immediately below the surface. It is significant that none is above the present soil surface, indicating the years that must have passed since the Aborigines conducted their feasts here. The shells littering the surface of the blowout below have been released from their burial place by the action of wind as it steadily expanded the area of the blowout. The shells are in an extraordinary state of preservation considering they are a minimum of 130 years old. One exposed turban shell I found had been eroded away to reveal the nacreous, or mother of pearl, inner layer, and it glowed in many different colours as the rays of the early morning sun picked up its strange whorled pattern.

The shells on the midden represent those that are still to be found in the rocks below – turban shells, limpets, abalone and mussels being the commonest. I photographed a group of shells next to a piece of chipped quartzite, which was almost certainly used by the Aborigines to remove the fish from the shell. Quartzite pebbles and flint are commonly found among the boulders on the beaches here and they were an important source

Plant bug (Coreidae) on eucalypt leaf.

of tools for the tribes who exploited the shellfish of the southwest coast.

Standing out starkly in the sand blows were some grotesquely twisted roots of old dead shrubs, probably Coast Beard Heath, which had been torn out of the sand by the savage winds. The abrasive action of the wind-borne sand had polished the roots and branches and this added to the surreal look of the blowout.

A small low outcrop of rock along Johanna Beach exposed at low tide revealed a large colony of sea squirts or, to use their Aboriginal name, cunjevoi. These strange creatures are members of the Ascidiacea, a name derived from the Greek meaning 'leather bottle', and they are aptly named. Long misunderstood and somewhat of a mystery, they are a member of the animal kingdom with a small tadpolelike creature as the immature phase of their life history, which eventually attaches itself to a rock surface and develops into the somewhat shapeless tough-coated adult that lives an immobile life, filtering sea water. They are highly prized by fishermen; I found quite a few that had been cut away for bait revealing the inner purple colour of the flesh. The squirts are only exposed at very low tide and when walked on, they surprise the unwary beachcomber with a squirt of saltwater. Nothing of the internal delicacy and colour of these creatures can be seen when they are exposed, but underwater the edges of the mouth are clearly visible.

Trudging back along the rock platform I saw a black and white spotted beetle settle on a rock. It was from the family Rhipiceridae whose members are characterised by relatively large antennae, somewhat reminiscent of the horns of a moose, but with a delicate fernlike structure. One wonders why the beetle should have such an extraordinary antenna; presumably it is to communicate with each other or to locate their prey. Apparently the life history of the Australian Rhipiceridae is not known but an American species is a parasite of the immature stages of cicadas.

A large plant bug of the family Coreidae settled on a gum leaf and made a good subject for a photograph with its bright orange and brown wing markings. These insects, like shield bugs or vegetable bugs, invariably emit a powerful odour. These odours are emitted from glands usually on the lower surface of the thorax from which the secretion spreads and evaporates; a surrounding roughened area prevents the secretion from spreading and covering the whole insect. The substances produced are both repellent to predators and toxic to other arthropods. In the case of the bug I photographed today, the smell was very strong indeed, perhaps

41

ABOVE: Freshwater crayfish (unidentified), Hopetoun Falls.

RIGHT: A cascading waterfall near Lavers Hill.

Summer scene at Moonlight Head.

somewhat reminiscent of eucalyptus oil.

The Hopetoun Falls today were in bright sunshine and small mayflies with long trailing appendages were silhouetted against the misty shafts of sunlight; perhaps it was their nuptial flight.

I photographed a very aggressive freshwater crayfish about 15 centimetres long which bit me and drew blood as I attempted to halt its progress across a rock. It was much darker than the larger blue crayfish I have sometimes found in the tributaries of the Murray River.

On the way home to Melbourne I photographed a potato field. The successive bands of colour made an interesting photograph – the white flowers of an earlier potato crop in the foreground, behind the deep green of a new crop, the red roof of a large old shed in the middle ground and with the blue of the foothills of the Otways and the lighter blue of the sky. The paddocks up here on the Otway Ridge have not really dried out this season because of the summer rain. At this rate they should look a picture by midautumn.

MARCH

LEFT: *An afternoon sea mist over Johanna Beach.*

ABOVE: *The Biscuit Star* (Tosia australis).

8&9 MARCH

I left home at midday. The weather was hot with strong winds from the northwest. The Western District is very dry but there is plenty of standing feed available for stock. The large round hay bales stand out in the paddocks and I guess it will not be long before they will have to be fed out to sheep and cattle.

Driving up the road from Birregurra through Forrest to Mount Sabine, I was interested in the way the wind moves the leaves of Satinwood trees. It rolls them over momentarily to reveal their silvery-white undersurfaces then, slackening, allows them to return and show their 'rightful' dark green colour.

I wandered about among a small patch of regrowth forest on Mount Sabine. It is surprising how clean and relatively bare it is under the closed canopy formed by Satinwoods, Hazel Pomaderris and Musk Daisy Bush. There is no sign of water ferns (*Blechnum* sp), nor is there much Forest Wire Grass. There are, however, many old logs covered with mosses and small ferns. It would be an excellent place for fungi in late autumn.

I found and photographed a yellow slime mould (*Fuligo septica*). This is not a true fungus. It actually moves slowly along as it feeds, and at maturity condenses and hardens into spore-producing organisms called sporangia. Slime moulds do not obtain their food directly from the wood or other decomposing organic matter they are found on, but from tiny food particles, such as bacteria and fungal spores, that the feeding portion of the slime mould (the plasmodium) picks up.

I visited Turtons Track hoping to take some late-afternoon photographs among the tree ferns and the Mountain Ash. Unfortunately, the very bright patches of sunlight and very deep areas of shade made photography difficult. However, I did manage some interesting backlit studies of the Kangaroo Ferns and lichens attached to the trunks and branches of the Myrtle Beeches. These ancient trees with their myriad, tiny leaves provided a beautiful, dappled light but, because of the sharp contrast between light and shade, this effect is hard to record.

Driving out of Turtons Track, I passed a 1.3-metre Tiger Snake as it attempted to cross the road. I stopped the car and it turned around slowly

Slime mould (Fuligo septica).

in an effort to return to the patch of buttercup from which it had earlier emerged. I approached the snake cautiously and at first it did not move and I was able to photograph it. The Tiger Snake had a background colour of light grey-green with bold stripes across its body. Eventually I got too close to it for the snake's composure (and my own!) and it slid slowly and silently into the dense green cover of buttercup leaves. Tigers are quite common here and you need to remain alert during the warmer months because they have a habit of sunning themselves on tracks and grassy openings in the forest.

Later in the early evening at about six-thirty, I drove down to Moonlight Beach to take some sunset shots. A huge flock of Silver Gulls was gathered on the beach a few hundred metres from the foot of the steps. I assume they must have been attracted to this spot by the masses of crickets which have been washed ashore and whose bodies were lying all over the beach. There were live ones still clinging to the rocks and on the cliff face. It looks as though a swarm may have been blown out to sea. Crickets occur in plague proportions from time to time in the Western District where they occupy cracks in the basalt soils during the daylight hours, emerging at night to do great damage to the pastures. I have not heard of them swarming like this and being blown out to sea before, but this certainly happens with plague locusts on occasion.

I disturbed the gulls from their feast and they made off in a great circling flight, providing some interesting photographs. Firstly they flew low above the waves, their stark white colour contrasting neatly with the blue of the sea; then, finally, they turned back into the sun. The difficulty here is to adjust continually the focus of a telephoto lens. As you take a series of photographs in quick succession, some birds will be in focus and others out. I am hopeful, however, that one or two of the shots will be successful.

I noticed an Australian Kestrel high above me on a rock shelf on the cliff face; it looked like a fledgling. There was no sign of any adult bird.

TOP: *Misty morning landscape, Phillips Track.*

ABOVE: *Fledgeling kestrel on the cliffs above Moonlight Beach.*

ABOVE: *A butterfly of the Otway forest - the Solanders Brown* (Heteronympha solandri solandri).

RIGHT: *Rural landscape, near Weeaproinah.*

The kestrel looked down warily at me, but scarcely moved. It would be very safe here from interference from any imaginable predator.

I stayed overnight at Lavers Hill and left after breakfast for Phillips Track and Triplet Falls. On the way there, I took some interesting landscape photographs looking southeast from Phillips Track about five kilometres from the turnoff. There were bold lines of fences and red-brown neatly ploughed paddocks, all strongly highlighted when viewed through the telephoto lens. The atmosphere was misty with the sun just starting to come through.

I spent a long time this morning at Triplet Falls. I was hoping to get uniform light across the moving body of water, but it is not easy here because the Myrtle Beeches high on the ridge intercepted the rays of the early sun and the cascading water varied from a blinding white to a soft creamy shade.

While I was waiting for a change of light, I saw a small stonefly on the rocks below and I hastily prepared to photograph it. By the time I had set up my close-up equipment and negotiated the slippery rocky crossing, of course it had gone! Such is the lot of an insect photographer.

Stoneflies are essentially insects of streams, particularly the creeks and rivers of the cool, temperate parts of Australia. In most species, the female lays eggs directly into the water and the nymphal stage develops from these eggs, passing through a series of instars, eventually growing into an adult stonefly. This is usually achieved in the space of one year, but in some species it may take as long as three years. Stoneflies are mostly dull coloured and well camouflaged. They are usually seen on rocks in streams after they emerge in the morning, and are seldom observed except by entomologists or naturalists looking for them.

Australia's stoneflies exhibit close ties with the stoneflies of New Zealand and South America. Presumably this relationship has to do with earlier geological periods when the landmasses were joined.

18&19 MARCH

I was a few kilometres southwest of Apollo Bay this morning when I stopped to examine a dead snake killed by a passing car as it crossed the road. It proved to be a female Copperhead; several baby snakes lay next to the body of the mother. The Copperhead is a viviparous snake, giving birth to completely formed snakes. I have noted several dead Copperheads on the roads down this way in recent months but have only seen two live ones. Judging by the number of dead ones on the road, they must be the commonest species of snake here, unless of course they are bolder and hence more vulnerable to passing traffic than other kinds of snakes such as the Black Snake, Tiger Snake and Brown Snake, all of which occur here.

Walking down the track to Rotten Point in the later afternoon, I disturbed an echidna which immediately began digging itself into the soft grey sand by the side of the track. It is surprising how echidnas can bury themselves and disappear from view within a few minutes. I took some close-up photographs of the long sharp barred spines. Unlike most native animals, they seem to have adapted to just about every environment within Australia and can be found from the inland desert country to the alps. One would imagine that several separate species might have evolved to cope with such a great range of environmental conditions, but it is the one species only which occurs throughout continental Australia and is known officially as the Short-beaked Echidna.

Immediately to the east of Rotten Point lies Dinosaur Cove where a team from the Museum of Victoria and Monash University and a band of enthusiastic volunteers have uncovered some very significant dinosaur fossils. The fossils have been recovered with great difficulty by tunnelling

ABOVE: Patterns in boulders on the beach.

BELOW: Dinosaur Cove.

The skull of a small dinosaur discovered at Dinosaur Cove. The enlarged optic lobes are unlike those of other members of this family of dinosaurs. Their unusual size suggests that this species may have been able to see in the low light conditions that must have occurred for much of the year then, 100 million years ago, in a latitude close to the South Pole.

horizontally into the rock of the cliff face a few metres above the pounding ocean waves rolling in from Bass Strait. I spent the evening at the expedition headquarters and listened to team leader Dr Tom Rich give an account of what they have discovered so far about the dinosaurs and the environment in which they lived.

The dinosaurs uncovered so far are principally herbivores belonging to a group called hypsilophodontids. They were relatively small, none of them being larger than an average human being and were preyed on by smaller carnivores, the theropods. Also present were a variety of fish, birds and turtles.

Considering that this part of Australia was then, 105 million years ago, a part of Antarctica and located 75 to 85 degrees south, it was surprisingly rich in animals and plants. So far over 150 different species of plants, insects and animals have been discovered and undoubtedly many more must have

50

inhabited this densely forested, cool, humid valley which eventually became part of the division between Antarctica and Australia as they moved apart during the disintegration of the ancient Antarctic continent, Gondwanaland.

The findings here parallel recent discoveries in Alaska where it appears small dinosaurs were permanent, year-round residents and they too must have endured a very cold winter and a period of several months of darkness. Enlarged optic lobes evident in the fossilised skull of a dinosaur found at Dinosaur Cove lend credence to the idea that they may have foraged at night during the winter moonlight. Clearly the climate then could not have been as cold as it is in regions of comparable latitude today which are ice-bound for months on end. Estimates of the temperature vary with the methods used. Those based on geochemistry suggest a very cold average temperature of minus 5 degrees Celsius but palaeoclimatologists, who base their findings on the study of fossils, claim a much milder 10 degrees Celsius as more likely. Effort is now being devoted to determining which estimate is correct to provide a better understanding of how the dinosaurs and other creatures lived in this prehistoric Antarctic environment.

The existence of extensive cliffs of Cretaceous sediments in southwest Victoria is indeed fortuitous. Fossil remains are quickly weathered and the shore platforms at the base of the cliff faces which are constantly being worn away exposing fresh surfaces provide an ideal location in which to identify the small and widely separated pockets of dinosaur bones. To date they have been found in ancient stream beds where the skeletons accumulated and which are now represented by narrow (less than 30 centimetres) layers of mudstone.

I decided to go to Point Campbell the next day to observe the mutton birds (Short-tailed Shearwaters) coming in to feed their young at Mutton Bird Island. I arrived in time to take some late-afternoon shots, backlit photographs of the translucent berries of Seaberry Saltbush. The bright crimson berries looked extraordinarily brilliant, glowing like so many rubies in the dense bunches which form at the end of upright stems above the grey-green foliage of the Saltbush.

The mutton birds did not appear until well after sunset and at first I was unable to see them. But by viewing the island from the east, looking into the glow of the setting sun now below the horizon, it was possible to see the fast-flying slender-winged birds. They wheeled and soared before landing to bring food for their chicks, hidden during the day in burrows.

Crested Terns.

Mutton Bird Island.

Fortunately for the birds, it is not possible for visitors to get onto Mutton Bird Island but in other localities where the rookeries are accessible, it is said that by day all is silent and you would have no idea of the presence of hundreds or even thousands of immature birds hidden in burrows beneath the ground. The adult birds leave again before first light to continue their search for food out at sea and before they can be attacked by prowling birds of prey.

Mutton birds have attracted much attention since the days of Matthew Flinders who on his epic voyage estimated that the flocks he saw near Three Hummock Island numbered over 100 million. The life history of the mutton bird is extraordinarily precise. They return after their nonstop 15,000-kilometre flight from the north Pacific in the last week of September, prepare their burrows and mate. Despite this huge journey the site chosen by an individual bird for its nesting burrow frequently remains identical over its lifetime.

The eggs are duly laid, a single one to each pair, in the last few days of November. The male and female take long turns in brooding over the single egg, with the male taking the first period of 14 days. After emergence of the chick in mid-January it is fed at first each evening following the adult bird's ocean foraging. Steadily the feeds become less frequent until they cease in early April.

The young birds fly north during the last week in April and the first few days of May to feed on plankton in the north Pacific Ocean. Huge numbers of young birds perish on this long journey and less than half are thought to return later in the year to their breeding grounds. Five years pass before the female mutton bird matures and lays her first egg and six years before the male finds a mate.

In some of the islands of Bass Strait an industry based on the harvesting of chicks has operated for many years. The number of birds killed is now controlled and seems to have had no serious effect on the overall population.

Originally the birds provided a major source of food for the sealers and fishermen in Bass Strait but these days have long since passed, and in more recent times mutton birds have been eaten by connoisseurs, the oil and fat used for industrial purposes and the feathers for down in sleeping bags.

21 & 22 MARCH

I left Melbourne at four this afternoon. The weather was very hot and dry for this time of the year and the forecast claims that it will continue this way for several days.

I spent an hour or so photographing the sunset at Point Roadknight, looking southwest towards the Point Addis lighthouse. As usual, the outline of the lighthouse was very hazy from the mist and spray thrown up by the waves. At low tide, the wide stretch of fine, smooth sand and its light covering of water provided some excellent reflections. It was possible to pick up the sun as a broad orange band on the wet sand, and also to see the reflection of the sand hills and the more distant Otway Ranges.

Save for a few seagulls, it was a very deserted beach. It seems strange that whilst you find seagulls about everywhere and at all times on these beaches, you will never come across their nests. In winter they fly away to breed, building nests among stunted vegetation on isolated islands and coastal prominences.

Later, after the sun finally set and I was on my way to Lorne, I stopped hurriedly to catch a most vivid postsunset scene just before Urquhart Bluff. The whole exposed sandy beach of the bluff, which is very wide at low tide, was a brilliant vermilion colour as was the sky itself, with the dark mass of the bluff silhouetted between the two brilliant patches of colour.

I spent some time the next morning at Urquhart Bluff examining the large clumps of tangled seaweeds recently washed in. They formed a ragged outline at the top of the beach where they had been left by waves at high

Capsules and seeds of Banyalla (Pittosporum bicolor).

tide. There was a great span of colour and shapes among the seaweeds today. Some were cylindrical, others foliar, fernlike or straplike. The colours ranged from pink through red, white, deep green, olive green, chartreuse, beige and even jet-black.

Some of these clumps of seaweed were more than a metre in diameter and half a metre in height, often a mixture of several species. There were large straps of Bullkelp with that typically smooth rubbery look and others with ribs running longitudinally along the surface. They make interesting subjects for photography because some are translucent and glow golden when viewed into the sun at a low angle. The kelp must come from much deeper water beyond the shore platform off Urquhart Bluff.

A host of small molluscs, mostly covered in slime, were browsing on the rocks at low tide. I photographed a tightly-packed group of minute mussels with small gastropods in attendance.

In the afternoon I took the Lorne Road to the Mount Sabine turnoff where there is dramatic evidence of the Ash Wednesday fire. There are huge dead eucalypts, 30 metres or more in height, but with much regrowth now coming through beneath them. There are also the remnants of a tiny pine plantation, all the trees having been killed. It is such a small group of pines that one would have to believe it is one of the school plantations that were favoured so many years ago. It demonstrates how vulnerable pines are in a bushfire and how they need to be adequately protected. There is no regrowth with pines after a severe fire.

Further along the Mount Sabine road I pulled into what must have been an old farmhouse site. There were some very large cypresses, a few garden plants and some open pasture rapidly being encroached by forest.

Two small butterfly species, the Silver Oreixenica and the closely related Kershaws Brown, were both about in numbers, enjoying the last rays of the afternoon sun. Early in the day you see the male Silver Oreixenica and the Kershaws Brown in solitary fashion; but as evening approaches and the shadows lengthen, they flutter about slowly at grass level. Eventually they team up to occupy the few small patches of remaining sunlight. Finally, small groups will select a suitable grass tussock, a rush or a frond of bracken on which to perch. Sometimes you may find as many as six hanging like so many Chinese lanterns from a single bent grass stalk. If disturbed, they fly about weakly and soon regroup on another suitable perch.

White Ibis silhouetted against a late afternoon sky.

I have often wondered why these butterflies behave in this way. They may in fact just be drawn together by their habit of pursuing the last rays of weak afternoon sun at a time of the year when most other species of butterflies are in their egg or larval stages. Or perhaps they gain some protective advantage by their gregarious behaviour – the sudden fluttering of many disturbed butterflies is likely to be more frightening to a potential predator than that of a single specimen.

I found some bright red open fruits of Banyalla, a form of pittosporum. The red seeds set between chestnut brown seed covers made a good study for close-up photography. Banyalla is closely allied to the common pittosporum grown in gardens, often as a hedge. The name pittosporum is derived from the words pitto (pitch) and sporum (seed). It is an apt name and the red seeds were very gluey when I touched them.

I headed back to Deans Marsh at 4.50 pm with clouds scudding over the crest of the Otway Range. A few kilometres beyond Deans Marsh, at a swamp immediately to the west of the road, I stopped to take a photograph of a large group of water birds. They were Sacred or White Ibis. The Ibis flew off quickly and settled on a large, dead tree. As a silhouette and shot with a 600 millimetre lens into the sun, this should produce a picture with little detail but hopefully some impact.

29 MARCH

I arrived at Point Addis this morning to a very powerful onshore wind and the car rocked to and fro as I waited for an opportunity for some photography. Point Addis, named after Superintendent EB Addis, Commissioner for Lands under Governor La Trobe, is an exposed promontory catching the full force of gales from the south and the southwest. Today I imagine the gusts would have been up to 80 kilometres per hour and there seemed absolutely no chance for any of the early morning shots I had hoped for.

Eventually, as the wind dropped, I emerged from the car and spent time examining the vegetation on this windswept precipitous coastline. The shrubs here are very stunted and misshapen and technically classed as salt-pruned vegetation. Eucalypts such as Messmates and Brown Stringybark that grow up to 20 metres in height a kilometre or two inland, here barely reach two metres. Smaller shrubs such as White Correa and tea tree literally hug the ground in a prostrate position, and old weathered and whitened limbs can be seen through their sparse foliage.

On the southeastern edge of Point Addis the land falls away steeply to the rocks below and the soil is held by grass tussocks, herbs and brightly coloured pigface (Rounded Noon Flower). The shiny swollen leaves of the pigface are now bright green and red. I have not observed this plant

ABOVE: Lichens (unidentified).

BELOW: The Dispar Skipper (Dispar compacta), a common butterfly in the late summer and autumn.

consistently enough to know whether this red colour is permanent or seasonal. Perhaps it is due to the formation of anthocyanin that accumulates as the weather becomes cooler and that colours the autumn leaves of deciduous trees and the bark of eucalypts growing at higher altitudes.

Among the dwarf shrubs I found a colourful group of lichens attached to a small dead limb of a tea tree. One of the lichens was bright orange and the other, a foliose or leafy type, was grey-green. The orange lichen displayed several prominent disks. These are apothecia, the fruiting bodies. Under a microscope it is possible to find in one layer of these fruiting bodies many spore capsules or asci, each usually containing eight spores. In this respect it seems to be a typical ascomycete or cup fungus. Yet combined with its partner, a species of algae that provides it with nutriment, it is in fact another creature, a composite plant, a lichen. The fungus, though providing some physical support to the algae, is for all practical purposes a parasite.

As I was examining the lichens, the sun suddenly and quite unexpectedly emerged as a large threatening storm cloud blew away. Instantly the huge bluff was brilliantly lit to a golden colour, and the more distant and crumbling cliffs at the head of the bay were starkly revealed. The sea, previously dull leaden grey, was transformed to sparkling azure blue with the long curving white lines of surf so characteristic of this bay.

I returned later to a nearby patch of heathy woodland I had visited last November to see what changes had taken place. Gone, of course, were the great diversity of spring wildflowers and in their place was a single flowering species, the Common Heath. However, there was some competition from the taller bushes of Dusty Miller. Although this plant appeared to be in flower, closer examination showed that the white colour was not coming from the flowers, which are still in bud, but from the strange dusted floral leaves which surround them.

The Common Heath in this particular locality is almost entirely pink and red with very little of the white variety. The species flowers for a very long period and will still be in evidence in the spring six months from now. Because it reaches its peak of flowering in winter when very few other plants are in flower, and because it is so abundant, Common Heath makes the greatest visual impact of all wildflowers. I have seen whole hillsides on the Anglesea heathland a mass of red, sometimes white, or a mixture of both. Although Common Heath, Victoria's floral emblem, also occurs in New South Wales, South Australia and Tasmania, nowhere have I seen it reach such density and such showiness as on the coastal heathlands of Anglesea.

I took some time to photograph a developing flowering spike of Silver Banksia. It is quite extraordinary the way in which the spike develops, and the changes in shape and texture that accompany this metamorphosis, before the dozens of tiny individual flowers emerge from the spike. Judging by the number of capsules I could find on old fruiting spikes, only a few of the flowers succeed in developing a capsule. It is said to be less than 10 per cent.

Nearby was a yellow flowering Prickly Geebung. Like Silver Banksia, this species is a member of the family Proteacea, which finds its greatest development in Australia with over 600 of the thousand-odd species occurring worldwide and which is represented in fossil beds in the Anglesea district which are 35 million years old. The flowers of the plants in this family are often small, highly variable in shape and colour, and provide one of the more exciting aspects of the Australian bushland. So much of the peculiarly Australian look of our flora depends on banksias, waratahs, grevilleas and hakeas.

The Proteacea are unusual among flowering plants in being represented in surprisingly similar forms in places as far-flung as Chile, the Cape Province of South Africa and southern Australia. Long before the advent of the theory of plate tectonics and a logical explanation for the idea of continental drift which now allows us to explain how Africa, South America, Australia and the Antarctic were once joined as the one supercontinent, Gondwanaland, Charles Darwin pondered how this might have occurred. He reasoned correctly that the ice-covered Antarctic continent must have once enjoyed a warmer climate and may have supported a highly peculiar and isolated flora. Although unable to offer a solution to this puzzle himself, he noted that 'the affinity' would no doubt some day be explained.

BELOW LEFT: Developing flowering spike of Silver Banksia (Banksia marginata)*, a prominent member of the family Proteacea.*

BELOW RIGHT: Another unusual member of Proteacea, Horny Cone-bush (Isopogon ceratophyllus) *which flowers in spring.*

APRIL

LEFT: *Mountain Ash* (Eucalyptus regnans) *and Blackwood* (Acacia melanoxylon), *Turtons Track.*

ABOVE: *Jewel beetles* (Cisseis sp) *on a leaf of the Austral Grass Tree* (Xanthorrhoea australis).

4 APRIL

The weather was very clear when I left home this morning at five-thirty. There was a good display of stars and it was surprisingly hot for this time of year.

I stopped briefly at the Anglesea River to look for water birds. There weren't many about, just the usual flock of Silver Gulls and a lone Pied Cormorant perched on a pole on the river, seemingly oblivious to everything, including two ducklings swimming close by.

Further up the river, I followed the paths through the partially cleared swamplands. It is said to be a good area for water birds but I noted only a pair of Masked Plovers which took off noisily as I approached, and wheeled around to strafe me before flying away over the swampland. Their aggressiveness might suggest that they were nesting nearby, though it seems early for this – they usually nest in spring.

They are yet another species of native bird to have responded positively to the dramatic changes in the Australian environment following European settlement. Cleared land is very favourable to Masked Plovers providing it is wet during the breeding season. They have now extended their range to occupy much of mainland Australia and in the process have spanned the original environmental barriers which led to the development of northern and southern races of the species.

BELOW LEFT: Meat ants (Iridomyrmex purpureus) seeking nectar from the flowers of Silver Banksia (Banksia marginata).

BELOW RIGHT: Wasp larvae (Symphyta sp) on eucalypt leaf.

Later, I made my way to the Bald Hills. A few dwarf specimens of Silver Banksia were in flower. One of the inflorescences, or bottlebrushes, had attracted a number of very active meat ants furiously engaged in looking for nectar, burrowing into the individual flowers of the bottlebrush and

Puffball (Pisolithus tinctorius*).*

emerging to seek new supplies of the sugary solution. They are not regular visitors to flowers in my experience and I wondered why they would be so attracted to this particular flower. Perhaps it is a function of season – a lack of other alternative food sources – or perhaps they were not seeking nectar at all, but rather other, less conspicuous nectar-feeding insects that I failed to observe.

The grass trees which top Bald Hills had today attracted a few insects. They were not in flower but the long, slender leaves often support insects. Probably the position of these plants on the highest point on the hill is an attractive feature. Most interesting and eye-catching of the insects were beetles of the genus *Cisseis*. These are members of the jewel beetle family (Buprestidae) with brilliant colouring like most species of the group. Australia is particularly rich in this family which contains perhaps the most beautiful of all beetles.

Many kinds of butterflies accumulate on hilltops. The males fight to establish their ascendancy and to attract females, who visit the peaks sporadically and then mate and return to their breeding grounds to lay their eggs. Some species of beetles, notably ladybirds, also gather on hilltops. Perhaps the Cisseis employ the same strategy to encourage the likelihood of mating where a species is widely scattered over an area and a chance meeting of the sexes is rare.

I stopped to examine some very large puffballs on the roadside east of Gumflat. Some were the size of a grapefruit and they had emerged from the hard gravel on the road verges without any apparent damage to the surface of the fruiting body. The sheer number of spores in puffballs, particularly in large ones, is staggering. It can exceed many millions and is one of the more bizarre examples of the seemingly wasteful and profligate features of nature in providing many more reproductive cells than would seem necessary to ensure the continuation of the species. The English mycologist, John Ramsbottom, in his book *Mushrooms and Toadstools*, quotes a calculation made by AHR Buller of the number of spores in a giant puffball (*Lycoperdon giganteum*) which measured 40 centimetres by 30 centimetres by 25 centimetres. He calculated that there were seven trillion spores (7,000,000,000,000) and if each spore produced a fruiting body of the size mentioned, end to end they would encircle the globe five times. If the next generation was also completely successful they would stretch to the sun and back and weigh 800 times the weight of the world! By what mechanism is this potentially horrendous breeding capacity held in check? Fortunately only a minute proportion of puffball spores do reproduce. If they were even reasonably successful, a small area like this would be totally covered by puffballs in the next season.

ABOVE: Bearded Midge Orchid
(Genoplesium morrisii).

BELOW: Toadstools
(Phylloporus *sp*).

8&9 APRIL

The evidence of an autumn break is everywhere to be seen. All the paddocks are green with a good length of grass, and farm dams are brimming with water. It is not quite universal, however, and further to the west and even at Lavers Hill (one of the best watered places in Australia, south of the Tropic of Capricorn) conditions are quite dry. An early break like this one means so much to the farmer. A good sole of grass on the ground at an early stage ensures the pastures' continued growth for weeks ahead as the days get shorter and colder. And for those who are planning to grow a crop of wheat, barley or oats, a good start for the young seedlings is guaranteed. Of all the uncertainties associated with farming in southern Australia, the timing of the autumn break has to be the most critical for it controls the amount of winter pasture and hence the feed available on the farm at the time of leanest growth. It dictates how much hay will have to be fed, the price the farmer gets for his store cattle in the autumn, and it has a huge influence on the yield of crops.

I had a look near Anglesea at some autumn orchids now in flower. I located many Parsons Bands with quaint, down-pointing white twin sepals, and three species of leek orchids. These are small autumn growing orchids; unlike many of the leek orchids seen in spring, they tend to various shades of brown and mauve, although the green in these specimens was still visible, particularly in the Sharp Midge Orchid. The name midge by which these orchids are popularly known stems from their insectlike appearance. I also found the Bearded Midge Orchid which, like the Sharp Midge, has several flowers on a long inflorescence but is more arresting in appearance because of the fringed petals and sepals of the tiny flowers.

ABOVE: Silver Gulls reflected in wet sand.

LEFT: Emerald moth (Chlorocoma cf assimilis).

The early autumn rains have ensured a good display of toadstools. One species looked like the Horse Mushroom which is closely allied to the common mushroom, although it is said to be less tasty. This mushroom is also very like the Yellow Staining Mushroom which frequently causes mild poisoning but has never been associated with a fatality, unlike some species of toadstools which occur in Europe. The yellow stain can readily be seen if the mushroom is bruised. Another characteristic of this unpleasant mushroom is the somewhat square nature of the cap in the immature or button stage.

At Urquhart Bluff in the late afternoon I spent time photographing a very large flock of gulls beautifully reflected on the great expanse of wet sand which acted like a giant mirror. The detail of each bird was so faithfully reproduced in the shining surface of the beach that it might be possible to turn the photographs upside down and achieve the same effect.

I watched for several minutes while a kestrel hovered high above the dunes that run along the beach, motionless except for an occasional shift in position and fast beat of its wings. The kestrel finally plunged down onto the dune sand but did not appear to catch any mouse or other small mammal. Kestrels eat insects too and perhaps it may have seen a grasshopper or cricket, both are about now. Their keenness of eyesight is remarkable and, from a human perspective, the capability to identify an insect a few centimetres in length from 30 or more metres above the ground seems incredible. There is no way we can know with certainty what a bird sees, but the evidence from observation suggests they can scan a large field of vision and rapidly absorb detail, whereas the human eye, even if it can match a bird in visual acuity, needs to select out and concentrate on small portions of the field of vision.

Last night I set up my gas lamp in a clearing in the heathy woodlands that flank the eastern side of the Ocean Road, five kilometres north of Anglesea. It was a warm enough night for moths and insects generally, and some were attracted to the light. These included two species of emerald moth; one entirely green with a white line running the full length from the head through the thorax to the abdomen and seemingly bisecting it, the other with a mottled green forewing which would make it very difficult to see when settled on a leaf.

Spiders came to the light as well. There was a small huntsman, something like a wolf spider and a very fast-moving scorpion. Scorpions, I have found, are extremely difficult to photograph because they will not stay still and scuttle away quickly like crabs. The scorpions you find here probably sting

ABOVE: Bullant (Myrmecia sp) dragging captured moth to its nest.

TOP RIGHT: Bullants (Myrmecia sp).

BOTTOM RIGHT: A spider that came into the light (Argoctenus sp).

but they seem too small to be of any real concern to humans.

A few bullants also joined me in the ring of light cast by the lantern and there were many nests of smaller ants along the paths in the woodland. I have often noticed these ants' nests by day: neat conical structures made from orange and yellow subsoil and standing out starkly from the dark grey colour of these sandy tracks. During the day you never see any sign of ants; they won't even emerge if you poke a grass stem down the entrance hole. However, by night it is a scene of intense activity with hundreds of ants coming and going from each nest.

Tonight it was evident that there were two different species, one ant being considerably smaller than the other, although the nests were very similar. Some of the larger ants had caught insects of various kinds, including a small swift moth with a bright silver band along the length of its forewings. They were dragging it away unceremoniously to the nest.

As a group, ants have an amazing capacity to utilise a habitat fully. A huge variety of ants may inhabit a small area of a few hectares and 150 different species have been recorded from the one locality in both the Australian tropic and temperate regions. Even on one fallen log there may be many nests of several different ant species.

Ants achieve this efficiency of utilisation by sharing the main elements of the habitat: space, time and food supply. Different species occupy the litter, others forage on the ground, while some concentrate on the leaves, stems and bark of shrubs and trees. Ants have learnt to 'time share' too, particularly in hotter drier environments – some are seen only at the hottest time of the day while others forage exclusively at night. Whilst some ants have specific food requirements and thus do not compete with other species, many are scavengers dependent on the same scraps available in the local environment. However, the size of food particles collected is very closely correlated with the size of the ants and large ants do not compete with medium size and small ants for the same food particles when a range of particle sizes is available.

13&14 APRIL

I took the road inland from Kennett River and made my way up to the Grey River reserve. Immediately above Kennett River there are excellent views of the Otway coast looking back towards Wye River. The picture was neatly framed by graceful Manna Gums but, as so often happens, it was ruined by telegraph wires!

I walked briefly up the telegraph line clearing and noted a few Shouldered Brown butterflies flying about. They are a common autumn species in the Otways and have formed a distinctive race or subspecies during the time the region has been isolated from the Central Highlands and Gippsland. There was little else in the way of insect life. The undergrowth species alongside the easement were plants such as Hop Goodenia, Wattle Matrush and Prickly Moses.

The Manna Gums, which are small with interestingly shaped branches, dominate the undergrowth which has been fired regularly. In fact, controlled burning was in progress yesterday and there was much smoke about. Certainly Kennett River is very vulnerable to any fire sweeping in from the west and fuel reduction burning is a necessity. However, it can result in a narrow range of plant species and in fact, here, perhaps surprisingly, it seems to result in a mainly grassy understorey. Usually one expects scrub to be encouraged by firing and grass to develop, if at all, only after a long period in the absence of fires. But where firing is very regular, as in this instance, the shrubs cannot obtain a foothold and grasses dominate the understorey.

The Grey River reserve is very picturesque with a backdrop of ramrod-straight and snow-white eucalypts that look superficially like Manna Gums but are said to be Mountain Ash. There are some excellent groves of tree ferns but those closest to the road were swept away in a flood some years ago. The decimated area has been replanted but it will be many years before the tree ferns return to their former impressive state.

Along a pathway in the reserve some very active, small, wirelike leeches emerged from the debris on the forest floor obviously seeking a feed. They 'stood' on twigs and leaves, their heads swaying ceaselessly and expectantly as though in anticipation of their good fortune. Happily, I was able to avoid them. Strangely, in all my wanderings in the Otways, I have not attracted many leeches, though I have heard said that they can be very bad in some fern gullies.

Leeches are members of the ringed worms (phylum Annelida) to which

The golden glow of dawn at Cape Patton.

earthworms also belong. However, leeches are much more active than their close relatives and they have chosen a very specialised mode of existence which relies on the sucking of blood. To achieve this position, leeches have developed extraordinarily sharp and efficient mouthparts which enable them to penetrate the skin of their hosts without them being aware of the onslaught.

To provide a continuous flow of blood, the leech secretes an anticlotting agent from secretory glands in the mouth, which also ensures that the blood does not clot within its own gut. They also inject a local anaesthetic since the wound is apparently not sensitive to iodine, an antiseptic normally guaranteed to produce a violent reaction when applied to even the tiniest cut.

Leeches have an unbelievable capacity to engorge blood – in some species up to 10 times their own body weight. The blood is slowly digested by the aid of symbiotic bacteria in the leech's intestine, a slow process which may take six months and which enables the leech to survive a further six months without another meal.

So not surprisingly, leeches have been endowed with extraordinary powers of detection to enable them to secure that very rare but vital meal. They respond very rapidly to a sudden reduction in light which might indicate a shadow cast by a passing animal, to scents emanating from chemicals in sweat, and to heat generated by animals.

I noted many small fish in the rock pools along the river which is now flowing very weakly. These fish, which ranged in length from a few centimetres to perhaps 20 centimetres, were galaxias – slender native fish that have no scales and move fairly quickly when disturbed. There are four species of galaxias in the Otways. They are apparently carnivorous though I do not know what they feed on.

There were many water beetles about in the pools today among the fish. They were very active but an odd individual would emerge from the water and sun itself on the rocks. They do this periodically, at the same time filling the space between the wing covers and the abdomen with air. I managed to photograph one such unsuspecting specimen. I wondered what adaptation of their legs enables these beetles to move so swiftly in the water. Apparently the tarsi, or feet, of the hindlegs or at least the last pair, are flattened and covered with hairs. In effect, they act as paddles. I was joined in my observations at one point by a friendly and inquisitive Yellow Robin.

Later I drove to a point on the Grey River Road where it joins the spine of the Otway Ranges on the Mount Sabine Road. At this point the loggers have burnt an area of recently milled ash. Virtually nothing appears to be alive; just bare earth and a mass of blackened logs lying along the ground. A number of isolated tall seed trees have been spared but all the smaller, understorey plants like Hazel Pomaderris appear dead. The only real sign of life I saw was one solitary blackened tree fern just developing its first, new, emerald-green fronds.

Though radical and controversial, it seems that this scorched earth policy may be the only way of milling ash and securing an even regrowth of young trees. Certainly past efforts at logging in the Otways without follow-

FAR LEFT: *Toadstools* (Coprinus disseminatus) *on the underside of a fallen trunk of Soft Tree Fern* (Dicksonia antarctica)*.*

LEFT: *Dead leaves of Hazel Pomaderris* (Pomaderris aspera) *and a fern frond in a rock pool, Grey River.*

69

up, either by burning or by clearing, have resulted in little or no ash regrowth even after 50 years. The problem in the Otways is that with very high annual rainfall and generally cooler weather, it is extemely difficult to select that very short period of the year dry enough for a burn and yet not at the same time too dangerous to risk starting a major fire. Research is currently being conducted into alternative strategies to secure strong ash regrowth and yet minimise the impact on the environment.

I stayed the night at Apollo Bay and headed off early at six o'clock for Cape Patton several kilometres to the northeast. It was still dark at this hour but there were plenty of stars and it gave promise of a good morning for photography. Cape Patton provides commanding views of the southwest looking towards Apollo Bay. In the opposite direction, the scene is interrupted by the very steep cliffs into which the Ocean Road has been cut.

On the way back to Apollo Bay I took photographs of the waves pounding into the rocks along the coast. It was very noticeable that the best waves come in groups of perhaps half a dozen or so, separated by a gap of smaller waves. There were some really majestic rollers this morning, developing into huge, curling waves and breaking 100 metres offshore.

I spent the remainder of the morning at the mouth of the Elliot River, a few kilometres southwest of Apollo Bay. This is certainly not a river by any normal interpretation of that word. Today, with little water flowing, it would hardly be classed as a creek. However, despite its insignificant appearance, the Elliot River, two kilometres inland from here, was the site of an important timber mill established in 1884 by the Apollo Bay Timber Company. Timber from this mill was used to supply sleepers for various railway lines and was also made into wooden blocks used beneath the paved sleepers in the City of Melbourne. Logs were brought down to a jetty at Point Bunbury near Apollo Bay by horse-drawn jinkers along a railway line. As with other Apollo Bay mills, it failed mainly from the difficulty and delays when loading timber onto boats in the exposed port.

Beyond the mouth of the river, however, the variety of the life on the shore platform and the rock formations was indeed fascinating. The seas today were wild and the seaward portion of the platform was continuously pounded and washed by huge waves. On one high, raised ledge, the wash from the waves passing over the top fell down like a shower over the sheer edge at its rear. Temporary ponding of water on this platform provided a reservoir for an almost permanent flow of small rivulets over the back

wall. On the top of the rock platform it proved a great spot to observe the tideline environment, the life style of crustaceans, seaweeds, chitons and gastropods as well as sea stars and barnacles. There were also large encrustations of the tube worm (Galeolaria) and dense clumps of tiny mussels. The surge of water over the rock surface every half minute or so provided some opportunity for photography but was possibly a little dangerous. At one stage my tripod disappeared beneath the foam!

The several heights of this rock platform must be the result of different levels of the sea in times past. There is at least two metres variation in the height between the highest and lowest shore platforms in this locality.

The mouth of the Elliot River is an excellent place to view the concretions and the honeycomb weathering of the rocks on this coastline. Some of the concretions have broken away leaving a cuplike feature which must originally have been a raised rim around the original concretion.

Large, water-worn boulders are strewn along the riverbed, 100 metres or so upstream from the entrance. Did the boulders come down the river, and were they tumbled smooth en route, or have they been shaped by the action of waves and later been hurled up from the sea in a past storm?

Autumn pastures overlooking Johanna Beach and Lion Headland.

Despite the miserable trickle of water in this river today, I think they have been washed downstream. The carrying or transporting capacity of a stream increases dramatically as the speed of water rises, and flash floods in this high rainfall country behind the Elliot River would be relatively common. Following long periods of heavy rain in the watersheds of steeply graded streams such as this one, the biggest boulders than can be transported vary up to the fifth or sixth power of the velocity of the stream. Thus a fivefold increase of the rate of flow of such a stream would enable it to carry objects over 600 times the mass of those carried by the normal flow.

25 APRIL

There was no surf today at Point Roadknight and hence no waves breaking over the shore platform. I have been hoping to get a good morning to photograph the breaking waves in the first rays of the rising sun. Point Roadknight, exposed to both the south and the east, is well situated to provide opportunities. So far I have been unable to pick the right set of circumstances, namely a very low tide at sunrise, a clear day so the sun can be clearly seen, and big waves. It may take quite a few more visits to put all these factors together at the one time.

I spent time photographing worm casts and the patterns formed by the tide ripples in the sand. Conditions were ideal to do this because the very wide expanse of flat reflective wet sand and the low angle of the sun accentuated the shadows cast by the ridges in the sand.

On the ocean side of Point Roadknight the shore platform was fully exposed this morning and densely covered with the seaweed Neptune's Necklace. There were some good samples of limpets, starfish and anemones in the rock pools just out of reach of the swell.

There were some splendid exposed examples of the holdfasts of kelp revealed between each breaking wave. The strength of these anchoring devices is quite remarkable and can be traced back to the fertilised spores or zygotes of kelp which attach themselves to a suitable rock surface.

Lacking the protective coat and food reserves of the seeds of land plants, the zygotes of seaweeds must be able to attach themselves quickly to a surface, and germinate, often in the turbulent watery environment of the intertidal zone. In one significant group that has been studied (Fucaceae) they do this by secreting a sticky jelly near the point of contact, the adhesive being a sulphated polymer of the sugar fucose. Rhizoids, or rootlike growths, then develop from the zygote, invading cracks and depressions to further secure a permanent hold on the rock, and at the same time secreting the adhesive jelly. In time the attaching jelly hardens as crosslinks are formed between the polymer molecules. In mature kelp, the holdfast must be capable of anchoring a plant up to 10 metres in length which flails incessantly in the breaking and receding waves.

Near where I had parked my car at Point Roadknight a small crop of quaint toadstools – Shaggy Caps – had sprung up from the grass. The long, almost cylindrical caps of the larger specimens were eight centimetres in length and, as the name suggests, covered with shaggy scales. In fresh specimens, the gills are almost completely concealed by the cap and can only be seen by picking the toadstool and looking downward along the stem. Before maturity the caps are white. But, as I saw today, in older specimens they soon turn black and eventually liquefy. I photographed one overmature toadstool rimmed with a band of liquefied black exudate. In a matter of hours it would be reduced to a stem with a blob of black tarlike material left on top.

Shaggy Caps are said to be very good eating and I took a couple home with me and cooked them in a frying pan with butter. They certainly tasted

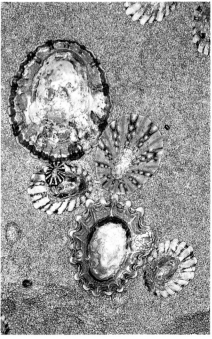

FAR LEFT: *Worm casts, Point Roadknight.*

LEFT: *Limpets (*Cellana tramoserica *and* Patelloida alticostata*) and a single small specimen of a false limpet (*Siphonaria diemenensis*).*

73

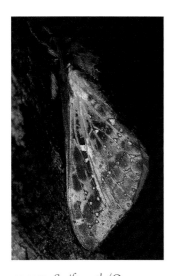

ABOVE: Swift moth (Oxycanus australis).

RIGHT: Neptune's Necklace (Hormosira banksii).

BOTTOM RIGHT: Holdfasts of Bullkelp (Durvillea potatorum).

excellent with a flavour more subtle than mushrooms. Luckily I did not have a drink with my meal because I have since learnt that alcohol and Shaggy Caps (and the related Inky Cap) are likely to produce an allergic reaction leading to nausea.

At a very small cove about 800 metres northwest along the beach towards Anglesea, I took photographs of some intricate dark coffee-coloured whorls in the yellow sandstone cliffs. Between this cove and Point Roadknight Beach the cliffs are made up of grey clay flecked with red, yellow and orange markings. It is a very unstable section of the coast. In places the cliff is giving way and falling onto the beach and the obvious and constant instability does not encourage you to venture too close. Nearer to the township of Anglesea the problem has become so serious that the area of worst slumping has been shored up by a large wooden barrier lest it continue too far inland and endanger houses.

In the sand at the foot of the clay cliffs patterns had been formed by the retreating tide, exposing the underlying ochreous rock and transporting jet-black sand, or rutile, into fernlike tracings.

Later, walking along the lonely shore, I was reminded of the virtual disappearance of the Anglesea surfing beach about 10 years ago. At the time this unfortunate event was the subject of much debate and people sought local man-made causes to explain it. Others recalled photographs and anecdotes from the earlier part of the century which indicated that the dunes behind the beach were then much lower than they are today. They wondered if it was part of a cyclical process.

One contributing factor could have been the wooden seawall situated half a kilometre to the southwest, constructed to prevent the continued slumping of the cliffs. Waves reflected from such a seawall tend to lower the beach face immediately in front of it; in turn this leads to an intensification of wave attack on the adjacent beach with a successive lowering of the beach profile to the east.

Recent studies demonstrate, however, that the disappearance of beaches is a worldwide phenomenon. Over 70 per cent of the world's sandy coasts have receded and only 10 per cent have built up in the last century. Coastlines in such remote areas as the Ninety Mile Beach of East Gippsland are receding and there is no evidence to suggest that this is connected in any way to human interference.

A small rise of a few centimetres in the world sea level during the last 100 years may have contributed to this massive removal of sand. A more significant reason is the general depletion of seafloor sand, a relatively recent process that has followed a very long period of deposition since the glaciers melted and sea levels rose between 1,800 and 6,000 years ago. Large quantities of sand were then delivered to the coast to build up beaches and dunes, but during the past 6,000 years this supply has gradually run out.

ABOVE LEFT: Shaggy Caps (Coprinus comatus*).*

ABOVE: A Shaggy Cap beginning to disintegrate.

MAY

*LEFT: The early morning sky casts
its light over the ocean at Bells Headland.*

ABOVE: Multicoloured seaweed.

5 MAY

It was very dark this morning as I left at five, with no signs of stars – a poor outlook, and that's how it turned out. It was a dull day, with intermittent rain and only fleeting bursts of sunshine. At Lavers Hill, low clouds continually scudded over the main range. Occasionally the sun would appear for a moment or two and then disappear for a much longer period.

For much of its length, the crest of the Otway Range is over 500 metres above sea level. As the first major land barrier to intercept the moist, prevailing southwesterly winds from Bass Strait and from the Great Southern Ocean, it forces them upwards, cooling them and causing the clouds to precipitate. Thus it is not surprising that the yearly rainfall on the top of the range averages 1,800 millimetres. In the low foothills of the northeast, the rainfall drops sharply away – due to a rainshadow effect – to as little as 600 millimetres. The Otway Ridge in effect steals the rain and leaves the land in its lee relatively dry.

I took more time to examine an abandoned section of the Great Ocean Road I had visited briefly some time ago. The rain that has fallen since my last visit has encouraged the appearance of many colourful toadstools and Bracket Fungi, but moving off the road surface to examine them proved to be very muddy underfoot.

Moving through the tree ferns and under the cover of the huge overhanging Mountain Ash trees, I was impressed by the sheer volume of rotting organic matter on the surface of the soil. In this very wet climate the rate at which eucalypt bark, leaves, branches and fern fronds accumulate is very rapid. This mulch also provides an ideal substrate for ground ferns and for fungi of many kinds.

It has been demonstrated that under Mountain Ash forests, over seven tonnes of litter per hectare may accumulate each year. Much of this humus is derived from the leaves of the Mountain Ash. The major leaf fall occurs in summer and early autumn, and so now the litter layer is at its thickest.

Rain clouds over the Otway Ridge.

LEFT: *Toadstool* (Laccaria *sp*).

BELOW LEFT: *Toadstools*
(Marasmius *sp*) *help break
down fallen leaves of Mountain
Ash* (Eucalyptus regnans).

The total weight of litter on the forest floor at any one time can be as high as 20 tonnes per hectare; the bulk of the organic material takes about three years to break down.

The rate of disintegration is greatest during late autumn and winter. By spring, when the warm weather dries it out, the litter can be seen to be thinner on the ground. Leaves decompose more quickly than twigs, bark or branches, and large logs or stumps may last for as long as 90 years before they finally vanish. In mature Mountain Ash forests, the leaves disappear within one year.

The organisms responsible for the conversion of this plant material to organic matter and its eventual return to the soil are many and varied. Insects of many types eat the green leaves, fungi attack the older remains of the vegetation, and springtails and earthworms play their part. Strangely, the Mountain Ash, which dominates the forest, returns less nutritious plant material than several of the associated understorey plants. Hazel Pomaderris, Musk Daisy Bush and a variety of other shrubs are important in providing the richer and more easily digested humus that sustains these giant trees.

An unusual fern occurring in the deep gullies in this area is the Skirted Tree Fern. Dead fronds are retained hanging down around the trunk (as

they sometimes are in other species). The Skirted Tree Fern, which was only discovered in 1940, was at first accorded specific rank; but in more recent years, the consensus of expert opinion is that it is a hybrid, a cross between the Rough Tree Fern and the closely allied Slender Tree Fern. Although its characteristics are consistently portrayed in most individuals, it has never been found in the absence of either of the suspected parent species.

I encountered a Black Otway Snail. A handsome species with a highly enamelled, jet-black shell, it is as big as an average garden snail but seemingly with nowhere near the same concern for potential predators. As I attempted to photograph it, the snail continued to move slowly across a mossy log with my camera held only centimetres away. The Otway Snail is strictly carnivorous, preying on earthworms, insect larvae and other small snails. You seldom see them in dry weather but cool rainy conditions brings them out. The distribution of this snail is confined to the wetter parts of the Otways. A closely allied species occurs in a similar habitat in the Central Highlands of Victoria but it can be readily distinguished by the bright orange colour of its footfrill.

There had obviously been a heavy wind storm in the last few days because the surface of the old road was covered with leaves and small branches from the tall Mountain Ash above. I am not certain that these were all Mountain Ash. They had the right shape, the leaves looked like those of a Mountain Ash and, although a poor diagnostic character, the trunks were very white and clean of bark almost to ground level. In this latter aspect some looked like very tall Manna Gums. Typical Mountain Ash has grey-brown bark which covers the trunk for up to 15 metres above the ground. I must find some buds and fruit to make a positive identification of these trees.

Looking up into this group of white-trunked giants, I tried to guess which was the highest. It is surprisingly difficult to do unless you are fortunate enough to be able to get well back from the trees, which is usually impossible because they grow in such close proximity, protecting each other against the ravages of wind storms. As soon as the supporting trees are felled, as happened tragically in the so-called Sample Acre of Victoria's tallest trees at Marysville, the remaining ones quickly deteriorate.

I doubt whether any of these trees would be much over 60 metres in height. They are regrowth trees possibly resulting from the devastating 1851 fire which is said to mark the birth of the very similar and famous trees along the nearby Turtons Track. Occasionally you find an ancient survivor, 300 years or more in age – like the well-known Big Tree at Melba Gully – but nearly all the Otway forest giants have long since gone. Although the big trees were ruthlessly destroyed by timber millers and settlers in their efforts to establish themselves in this very difficult environment, there was also an element of local pride in these forest giants. A number of black and white photographs taken before the turn of the century show pioneers linked hand-in-hand around the enormous buttressed trunks or posing outside rough dwellings made from giant stumps.

As part of the World Exhibition in Melbourne in 1888, a reward of £20 was offered to anyone who could locate a tree of 400 feet (122 metres) or more in height, with £3 for every extra five feet. The idea was to exhibit photographs and physical details of the trees in the Royal Exhibition Building. The organisers fervently hoped that it would be possible to find a tree which exceeded the world record of around 350 feet (107 metres), attributed to a Redwood in California. Although tales abounded of local trees of 500 feet (153 metres) in height, in fact the tallest discovered was 326 feet (99 metres). It was located on the slopes of Mount Baw Baw in Gippsland and its height was determined by theodolite measurement.

The details of the seven tallest trees were exhibited in an atlas entitled *The Giant Trees of Victoria*. The Otways had a sole representative among the seven chosen but of the somewhat disappointing height of 290 feet (88 metres). However, another record in the Fifth Progress Report of the Royal Commission on State Forests and Timber Reserves of 1898 claimed a fallen tree had been measured at 329 feet (100 metres) to the point where it was broken off and must therefore have been even higher in its original standing state. This tall tree was known as the Olangalah Tree. Another Otway giant was measured having a girth of 64 feet 6 inches (19.67 metres), eight feet (2.4 metres) above the ground.

In this age of sensitivity to conservation issues and to the preservation of forests in particular, it is interesting to record the thoughts of a Mr EJ Dowey who led the party to the Mount Baw Baw tree. He later recalled how much timber the local splitters had obtained from that particular stand and casually remarked that the 326-foot tree yielded 6,000 six-foot lengths of palings. So much for conservation in 1888!

Although the Otways did not officially claim the tallest standing tree, there is evidence that the district had some of the bulkiest. The stump of a tree which was retained for many years in the local showgrounds at Beech Forest, before it too disappeared in one of the numerous fires,

FAR LEFT: A flower of Southern Blue Gum (Eucalyptus globulus) emerging from the bud.

LEFT: Flower of Southern Blue Gum (Eucalyptus globulus).

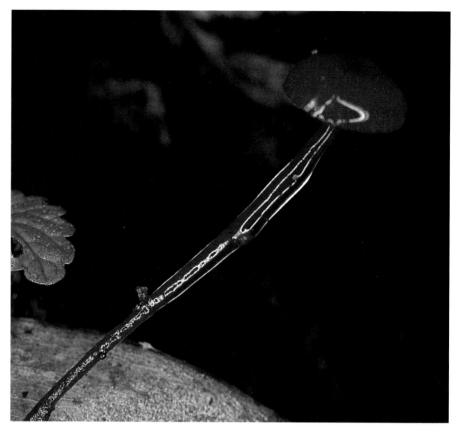

was known as the Bandstand. It is recorded that the Governor of Victoria, Lord Hopetoun, and his party on a visit to the town, danced the quadrille on a stand on the top of the stump at an evening function held in his honour.

The great number of fallen leaves made an interesting subject for the camera with colours ranging from crimson, through orange, yellow, brown and bright green. A variety of fungi, particularly small toadstools, contributed to these vivid hues. I saw several which I took to be individual species, since agarics (toadstools) are notoriously hard to identify unless you examine the spores under a microscope. But one was unmistakably the beautiful blue Pixie's Parasol. I have nearly always found this small delicate toadstool on dead eucalypt trunks, usually those in a relatively good state of preservation. It never ceases to amaze me how the hyphae, or fungal roots, of so delicate a fungus can invade such a seemingly hard and intractable substrate. Another species of the same size and the same genus (*Mycena viscido-cruenta*), which is a small brilliant red toadstool, retains a layer of glutinous liquid around the stem. The bright red species has to be handled with great care; not only is it very fragile but it seems always to grow on small twigs and pieces of dead fern which are all interconnected. As soon as you put your hand on the ground or perhaps your knee, it is likely to set off a chain reaction which often results in the destruction of a tiny fragile toadstool half a metre away.

Driving home through Lavers Hill and Weeaproinah this afternoon, I was again struck by this beautiful, peaceful rural scene. Maybe because of its intense greenness and the gently rolling hills, it reminded me of places elsewhere, perhaps the Downs in England. Certainly nowhere in Victoria, or in fact mainland Australia, does any locality maintain such an appearance of lush greenness for so many months of the year. It is not surprising, therefore, that this is an ideal area for dairy production, suffering only by its distance from the major domestic market in Melbourne. Again because of its excellent growing climate and its isolation, this section of the Otways was selected for the production of disease-free potatoes.

9 MAY

This morning, on the road up to the main Otway Ridge from the little town of Gellibrand, I noted several plant species pioneering recently cleared and burnt country along the roadside. As well as Blackwood, which so often dominates new vegetation in the high rainfall forests of the Otways, in these drier and more open forests there was evidence that other shrubs such as Christmas Bush, Hazel Pomaderris and Dogwood play a significant early role in the re-establishment of the forests.

Higher up in the heavier forests are the Satinwood. They grow into small well-shaped symmetrical trees up to 20 metres in height, and are easily recognisable. Satinwood is a member of the genus *Phebalium* and is closely related to the boronias. Many of these plants have highly aromatic leaves and Satinwood is no exception. When the leaves are crushed, they emit a strong, pungent odour which is not entirely unpleasant. Unlike most other phebaliums which have yellow flowers, Satinwood has clusters of white starlike blossoms which make it a most attractive tree during the spring months. The timber, which has been described as pale, hard and dense and somewhat resembling English Box, was used years ago in veneers for carving and cabinet woodwork and I have been told it was also a source of wood for the old school rulers.

Perhaps the most interesting thing about Satinwood is its unusual distribution. Although it is widespread and very common in the better watered parts of the Otways, it is only represented elsewhere in Victoria by a much smaller and round-leafed variety, restricted to Mount Elizabeth in Gippsland. However, it again occurs in the same larger tree form around Sydney and is also very common in Tasmania. Why doesn't it grow in the closely similar high rainfall forests east of Melbourne?

Later at Melba Gully I spent a few hours photographing the ferns and mosses and a tiny waterfall cascading past a solitary Soft Tree Fern. Looking up into the sun filtering down through the myriad tiny leaves of the Myrtle Beech canopy, I was struck by the great number of epiphytic ferns clinging to the limbs of these ancient trees. They are mostly Kangaroo Ferns, so called because of the spreading leaflike fronds which sometimes look like the foot of a kangaroo. Frankly I think this connection is far from obvious and must leave many visitors in a quandary as to how the name was derived.

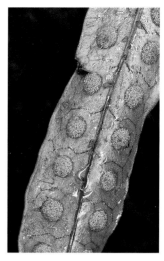

ABOVE: Spore-containing bodies (sori) on the lower surface of a frond of Kangaroo Fern (Microsorum diversifolium).

BELOW: Kangaroo Fern (Microsorum diversifolium).

Even the Latin name of this fern – *Diversifolia* – highlights the variability of frond shape. Some of the ferns were perched precariously on branches 25 metres above the ground. They seem to favour beech trees, perhaps because the bark of this species is softer, decays more easily and provides a suitable local habitat for the rhizomes of the fern. Unlike many other ferns, the Kangaroo Fern fronds vary in colour and, silhouetted against the sun, the subtle shades of light green, amber and pink provided an attractive contrast to the dense greenness of this gully.

I noticed some scratching along the sides of the pathway and my instinctive thought was lyrebirds; but these birds do not occur in the Otways. Why is this so? Only a week ago I was walking in Coles Gully in the Dandenong Ranges, east of Melbourne, and I saw and heard lyrebirds, although they are not nearly as common or as tame as they used to be because of the increase of dogs, cats and foxes. It seems strange that a bird which occurs down the Dividing Range of the east coast of Australia, from southern Queensland to within 40 kilometres of Melbourne, has not made the extra 100-kilometre jump to the seemingly ideal habitat of the Otways. The answer probably lies in the isolation over a million years ago of the Otway forests from those of eastern Victoria by the formation of the volcanic plains, and the lower rainfall that exists between these two well-watered regions. Presumably the lyrebird developed and spread its range to southeastern Victoria after the connection between these two similar habitats had been broken. The lyrebird is also absent from Tasmania and this would suggest its appearance in southern Victoria may have been quite recent since a land bridge between Tasmania and the mainland existed only 10,000 years ago; although at that late stage the connecting country would probably have been unsuitable to support the lyrebird. It may well have inhabited southeastern Victoria at the time the land bridge existed, but the connecting sand bars between Wilson's Promontory, the Bass Strait islands and Tasmania would have been a mostly sandy, inhospitable habitat for a shy bird of the forests.

The absence from the Otways of the Sassafras, that highly aromatic and attractive tree of eastern Australian fern gullies, is also a puzzle. Unlike the lyrebird, Sassafras is represented commonly in Tasmania and also occurs on King Island, less than 100 kilometres from Cape Otway. Sassafras is very susceptible to fire and it has been suggested that it may have been eliminated from the Otway Ranges by a huge wildfire or a series of smaller fires. Although there is no doubt that the Otways have been subject to repeated bushfires over thousands of years, fire seldom completely destroys all vegetation, particularly in deeply dissected country which is where you would expect to find Sassafras. Even the most devastating of fires will leap some gullies leaving small remnants of scorched but relatively undamaged vegetation.

I was surprised later this afternoon to see a number of Silver Oreixenica butterflies flying in the weak afternoon sunshine. It is now very late in the season for this dainty little species with their prominent eye spots and striking silvery markings to be on the wing. It first appears here in March and usually has all but gone by mid-April, the females by then having laid

The moon rises over a potato field near Lavers Hill.

85

The aftermath of the Ash Wednesday fire of February 1983, near Big Hill.

their eggs on grass, usually one of the tussock grass species.

On the way home today, I took some photographs of the gently rounded hills near Weeaproinah. One of my photographs included a huge solitary dead trunk of a Mountain Ash still standing in a paddock by the roadside. It may have been ringbarked by settlers or perhaps killed by fire. It made me think about the devastation that fires have caused in the Otways since settlement and how they have shaped and influenced this region.

Although records of the earliest fires are very limited, there is little doubt that the Black Thursday fire of 6 February 1851 was more devastating to the vegetation of the Otways than any that has occurred since. It was so hot and so fierce that it burnt out some of the wettest and most luxuriant gullies, including those along Turtons Track which have not been burnt since. Though of a much greater magnitude than the Ash Wednesday fire of 9 February 1983, there was very little property damage and no loss of life. This was simply because a mere handful of settlers had by then reached the Otways. It is recorded, however, that the newly established township at Apollo Bay, then known as Middleton, was almost wiped out and that the few inhabitants were forced to shelter on the beach.

The cause of this fire is generally attributed to burning off by recently arrived settlers in the Western District. Without previous experience of the ravages of bushfires they burnt off the dead and cleared timber on their properties during the summer months, blissfully unaware of the danger that lay ahead. Then, almost inevitably, a hot northwest wind sprang up early in February and swept these farmland fires across the grasslands to the foothills of the Otways and finally into the tall dense forests.

11 & 12 MAY

I arrived at Urquhart Bluff at 11 am. It was cloudy and windy and no one was about, just me and a great stretch of lonely and deserted beach. I attempted to film the extraordinary banded rocks which occur here. I guess they must be sedimentary in origin. The bands are of different colours and textures – pink, mauve and cream – but somewhere along the geological way, they have become hopelessly jumbled and twisted, as though the soft rock has been subject to immense pressures. We have always called them the candy rocks, because they have the appearance of an old-fashioned boiled sweet. One explanation as to how these coloured bands were formed is that they result from a regular, perhaps seasonal, variation in the iron oxide precipitation from ground water solutions. There have been earth slides and they look to be very recent. Probably the result of these last rains. This country is very unstable and the coastline is continually being eaten back.

The tide was well out when I set out to walk around the bluff to the big rock pool. The exposed rocks were very greasy and quite dangerous to walk on and I fell once or twice.

The salt spray has been very active in recent weeks; there is much burning off of the vegetation in the amphitheatre between the first point, Urquhart Bluff and the rock pool. With the skeletal remains of the old Moonah bushes and Coast Beard Heath, it is a very harsh landscape. Beyond this landslip section, tussock grass (*Stipa* sp) and a variety of herbs cling precariously to narrow shelves on the high, yellow cliffs.

A White-faced Heron alighted at the edge of the pool and stalked cautiously around its edge. It was revealing to watch this tall, slender bird seeking

ABOVE: Banded rock at Urquhart Bluff resulting from seasonal variation in iron oxide precipitation from ground water.

*BELOW: Coastal Moonahs (*Melaleuca lanceolata*) shaped by the incessant on-shore winds.*

FOLLOWING PAGE: A late afternoon haze over the Twelve Apostles.

ABOVE: *White-faced Heron.*

BELOW: *A wave breaks over rocks at Point Sturt.*

out marine creatures, suddenly arching its neck then craning it forward to examine the rock surface more closely and then, in its slow, stilted walk, moving on again.

I also photographed a solitary Little Pied Cormorant perched on the rock above the waves at the sea edge of the shore platform. It made an interesting study against the stormy sea and the line of distant cliffs reaching down to the Aireys Inlet lighthouse. Like all cormorants, they have the habit of raising their wings to form a coathanger effect when viewed head on or from the rear. They do this when resting to dry their wings.

Later I parked my car a few hundred metres beyond Cinema Point and made my way down a very steep and narrow path to the beach, perhaps 100 metres directly below. The beach is broken up into a series of small, sandy crescents between rocky outcrops. Exposed to the southerly gales, it is obviously a very turbulent environment and at high tide the waves reach the base of the cliffs. There are numerous thick deposits of broken shells in the sandy sections. These are dominated by limpets of many colours and patterns. However, from their general appearance and uniform shape, they mostly belong to the one species (*Cellana tramoserica*). I found the remnants of a few larger shells, including abalone and scallops, but the bigger shells are soon broken up by the continuous pounding of the heavy surf.

Shells accumulate on beaches close to large populations of living shellfish, in estuaries, on rock platforms or near offshore reefs. Sometimes the shells are trapped, as they were at this beach, by raised bands of rock, and the deposits may be quite deep. The shells tend to be graded both vertically and laterally by the action of the breaking waves. I noticed how the larger shells lie on the surface and smaller ones beneath. The forward movement of the breaking wave, the swash, pushes shells up the beach but much of its power is lost as water seeps quickly into the sand. The retreating phase of the wave, the backwash, leaves very large shell fragments behind at the top of the beach but washes the smaller fragments back towards the

sea and ensures that the finest of these fragments find their way downward into the lower levels of the shell bed.

I stayed overnight at Lorne and rose early to take some dawn photographs at the picnic area immediately southwest of the town. Sunrise was unimpressive because of the low sea cloud but sufficiently bright to produce some moody reflections on the very smooth and glassy shore platforms. The shore platforms here hold very shallow pools of water, in places scarcely a centimetre deep, between the upraised edges of the cracks which crisscross the surface and divide the flat rock ledges into a variety of geometric shapes, often pentagons. The rock immediately adjacent to each crack is oxidised to a lighter colour and must be harder, since in the process of the erosion they are left as ridges and some water from each receding wave is retained as though in a series of very flat trays.

On the Ocean Road just south of Lorne above the mouth of the Saint Georges River, I took time to photograph some striking backlit cloud formations. I was able to pick up the reflections of these clouds in the very shallow lagoon at the mouth of the river. While recording this scene, a fox trotted unconcernedly along the beach and through the shallow water of the lagoon. I noticed footprints yesterday and I have previously seen signs of foxes at Moonlight Beach further to the west. The foxes presumably find fish or dead birds that have been washed in.

Recent research work involving the radio marking of foxes living in suburban Melbourne has greatly extended our understanding of the habits of this most resourceful animal. Far from an animal living by successfully stalking large live prey such as rabbits, birds and possums, foxes in fact have been shown to eat a huge range of materials ranging from scraps from rubbish bins, carrion, insects of many kinds, fruit, rats and mice.

22 MAY

I was on my way down to Bells Beach in pitch darkness at five o'clock. When I arrived the weather was quite clear and surfers were already in the water, visible as dark, almost ghostly shapes.

The powerful waves and spread of the foam looked striking and it picked up the reflections of the pink, dawn light. I wonder what combination of suitable conditions favours the production of these famous waves which have established Bells as one of the world's great surfing beaches. Clearly it faces the right direction, exactly catching the huge ocean swells that ride in from the southeast. But the size of the waves and the evenness of each line of breakers is not reproduced at any of the neighbouring surfing beaches which have a similar aspect. The waves which roll in from deep water are intercepted by a rock floor which sweeps north along the shoreline, and causes the waves to break successively in a long sweeping arc. Having a rock base, Bells is not so subject to change as are so many other beaches along this coastline.

Later I stopped at the patch of heathland near Anglesea I have been examining on my previous visits. The Myrtle Wattle is just beginning to flower and there were some striking light effects created by the sun's rays shining through the multicoloured phyllodes, which most people would mistake for leaves. I took a photo of a single phyllode against the sun, the main vein being clearly visible in the silhouette created, as were the unusually thickened leaf margins, both standing out as bold white lines on a yellow and green background. Although the phyllode of a wattle looks like a leaf, it is in fact a thickened stem of an earlier true leaf, a feathery or bipinnate structure which occurs in all wattle seedlings. In Myrtle Wattle and many other species, the true leaves disappear to be replaced by a phyllode.

ABOVE: *Sunlit leaf of Myrtle Wattle* (Acacia myrtifolia).

BELOW: *The first rays of early morning sun creep towards Bells Beach.*

Later at Lorne Forest Park the effects of the autumn rains were clearly evident. Not only was the She-oak Creek running strongly but fungi of all sorts and sizes were out in abundance. The best conditions for these undoubtedly occur with early autumn rains. With effective rain falling between mid and late April, the ground is warm enough to promote the development of the fruiting bodies, that part of the fungus that attracts the eye. The bulk of a fungus is made up of the mycelium, or fungal roots, which remain invisible during the year, either underground or in rotting timber which eventually breaks down to organic matter. Unlike flowering plants which mostly flourish in spring, most fungi, and particularly toadstools, save their displays till autumn. There are some species that appear in the fruiting stage in the spring but this is not nearly as interesting to the naturalist

or photographer as autumn when most of the colourful toadstools, Cup
Fungi and Bracket Fungi, suddenly appear following the first good rains.

One toadstool I found was a violet cortinar. The cap had expanded fully
and the cortinar or veil that hides the gills in the early stages of development
had broken. Another species that attracted my attention was a large Bracket
Fungus (*Coltricia* sp) at the base of a burnt tree. Large droplets were suspended
at the end of the bracket, a feature I have often observed but have difficulty
in explaining. Could it have something to do with the transport of the
spores in this species?

A quaint-looking Parasol Fungus also caught my eye. It was not as obvious
as the other toadstools because the colour of the cap was subdued in shades
of grey, white, beige and brown, and it was almost camouflaged. What
gave it away was the white stem or 'handle' of the parasol. Parasol Fungi
have a characteristic and easily recognisable shape and a very prominent
annulus, the ring on the stem marking the point where the expanding cap
in its button stage breaks away as the growing toadstool expands.

One huge mass of tiny toadstools I photographed (*Coprinus* sp) exhibited
considerable variation in colour and shape within the one colony. The caps
of this particular species were ribbed and within the group the colour varied

considerably with age, emphasising the problems one has in positively identifying agarics without resorting to microscopic examination of the spores.

Several red-topped toadstools (*Russula* sp) had pushed up through a mass of leaves and sticks on the ground. It is surprising that such soft and delicate fungi can lift such large branches. In one case, the cap of the russula was covered in dirt, leaves and small twigs, with a single large fruit or gum nut of a Messmate sitting on top. The force of the expanding toadstool stems from osmotic pressure generated as water moves into the body of the fungus and swells the tissue.

I also found the dainty red-capped and white-stemmed *Collybia elegans* and one huge group of minute toadstools hiding under a log lying over the track. Another very attractive species was *Crepidotis*, predominantly white in colour, but at this stage it was being attacked by another species of fungus which left furry white mildew on the stem and on the cap. A pink Coral Fungus was an interesting find. It was a species of the genus *Ramaria*. These fungi, unlike Bracket Fungi and toadstools, have their spores covering the whole of the fruiting body; there are no gills or pores.

Later in the afternoon, walking down through the light undergrowth to a point on the Erskine River above the falls, I was struck by the way in which they suddenly appear, unexpectedly. The gradient above the falls is quite gentle. The reason for their appearance is the existence of a very resistant layer of rock, in this case a band of sandstone. The frequency of these hard bands in the sedimentary rock accounts for the unusual number of waterfalls found in the Otways. Many still remain to be discovered by the general public and in some cases even by intrepid bushwalkers because of the steepness of the gullies and the very dense understorey of plants that surround them.

The weather by then had clouded over which, rather strangely, is an advantage in the photography of deep fern gullies and waterfalls because the range of light values is manageable and it is also possible to capture the movement of the water by time exposure. Erskine Falls has a tidy appearance with trees and tree ferns framing the cascading water and making it easy to photograph. It is often very difficult to capture the beauty of some of the more remote and isolated falls in the Otways because of the surrounding undergrowth and the impossibility of getting far enough away to capture the whole scene.

Gills of a violet toadstool (Cortinarius sp).

Flowers of Red Ironbark
(Eucalyptus tricarpa).

31 MAY

Although it rained heavily during the night, when I left home at 5.15 am the stars were out, albeit among dark and stormy clouds. I arrived at Point Addis as the sun was rising and made my way down to the beach. The beach is very slightly shelving and when the tide retreats, huge expanses of sand are exposed. Today the tide was the lowest I have experienced here and a vast area of smooth sand was revealed, broken in places by partly submerged boulders of ironstone.

I watched a Pacific Gull. It took off majestically from the sand and wheeled around, very deliberately flying along the edge of the cliffs, black-tipped wings beating slowly and bright yellow bill proudly displayed.

The Red Ironbarks, the dominant tree in the basin behind Addis Bay, are now fully in flower. Many of the flowers, often still attached to small branches, have been broken off by Yellow-tailed Black Cockatoos and Crimson Rosellas. Those still on the tree were attracting honeyeaters, mainly Red Wattlebirds that chattered noisily as they fed on the nectar.

For a eucalypt, the Red Ironbark flower is very large and showy, with long yellow stamens and a pink style. The dark, hard bark of this tree is equally singular, being deeply furrowed and quite unmistakable. I have always thought it a strange tree to find in this part of Victoria, which is its most southern occurrence. Red Ironbark is much more typical of the goldfields country of northern Victoria and there it sometimes occurs in an unusual form with bluish leaves instead of the commoner dark green colour. Recently this northern form has been accorded specific rank and so there are now two separate species.

Bark type is one of several characteristics that have been used in the past to classify eucalypts, a very large and complex group of plants. Where a species starts and where it ends has been the subject of continuing debate in botanical circles for over 100 years. Eucalypts, unlike that other great Australian plant group the acacias, do not always fit neatly into the concept of a species and this has led to a search for a more satisfactory system of classification. The earlier use of bark and other simple characteristics for identification has now been rejected as being too narrow. The most modern system utilises a wide range of features, including the traditional ones such as bark and flower structure, but also takes into account the nature of the pollen grains, the essential oils contained in the leaves, the wood and many other characters.

At Point Addis it is intriguing to see how entire sections of the stunted coastal woodland have managed to survive after falling with their attendant soil down the cliff face in the periodic landslips that have occurred. In one example, a whole miniwoodland has apparently slumped almost vertically down the cliff face and yet it continues to grow only a few metres above the beach as though nothing has happened. In some instances, subsidence has carried plants that naturally inhabit the clifftops to the very edge of the surf, where in time they will surely be washed away in one of the occasional storms that lash the coast.

The Ironbark Basin behind Point Addis beach has been severely burned in recent years, notably in the Ash Wednesday fire. As a result, a very dense understorey of regrowth Varnish Wattle has sprung up, choking out almost all other shrub species. This has led to a relatively impoverished flora, although I have no doubt that in the absence of further fires, and as the Varnish Wattles mature and ultimately die, many species now rare will reappear in numbers. Sometimes fire is required to reveal the existence of certain species in mature vegetation. It is interesting to recall that the virtually complete removal of vegetation by the 1983 fire from the very well-known and closely observed heathland at Anglesea led to the reappearance of one species – Wrinkled Buttons – thought to have become extinct in this district and which had not been recorded for over 60 years. Despite initial fears, all but one species – the very rare Elbow Orchid – out of a total of more than 600 appeared to have survived this extraordinarily hot fire, which in many places left absolutely nothing but blackened tree remains on the ground. Just recently the Elbow Orchid has reappeared in its original haunts.

A great variety of seaweed had been washed up on the beach. There was a fascinating array of shape and form, with specimens that resemble coral, slices of lettuce, even one that looked like a dark green form of spaghetti, and the familiar broad, rubbery strips of kelp. Much of this seaweed had been rolled up in tangled, multicoloured heaps by the waves and left at the high-tide mark. It made me think about where this huge mass arose and how seaweeds relate to terrestrial plants.

Seaweeds are in fact algae, officially classed as marine algae and with a simpler and more primitive structure than the earliest forms of land plants

A green seaweed, Sea Lettuce (Ulva lactuca), and Neptune's Necklace (Hormosira banksii), a brown seaweed.

Bullkelp (Durvillea potatorum).

such as mosses and ferns. Seaweeds have no roots, stems or leaves, but merely a single vegetative structure known as a thallus. The thallus is held by a holdfast equipped with an adhesive plate which enables it to grip the rocks or other objects on the seafloor. Whereas land plants extract carbon dioxide and oxygen from the atmosphere through stomata or pores in their leaves and take up nutrients from the soil by their roots, seaweeds derive their whole requirements from sea water, including oxygen and all nutrients.

One of the reasons there are great accumulations of seaweed next to rocky sections of coastline is simply that rock provides a secure foundation for them. Some species adapt to sandy or muddy seafloors but are invariably found attached to small rocks, shells or sometimes to things thrown in by man, such as bottles or tyres. Seaweeds reach their maximum development and greatest diversity in cool waters – you don't notice them so much in the tropics. Most species are found at a distance from the shoreline and in deeper water. Under these conditions, some seaweeds attain enormous size, and kelps over 100 metres in length have been recorded, although Australia's largest species, the Bullkelp, seldom exceeds 10 metres.

The colours of seaweeds have been used to classify them into three broad groups: the green seaweeds (Chlorophyta), brown (Phaeophyta) and red seaweeds (Rhodophyta). Unfortunately, like so many simple methods of classification, it does not always hold true. What is scientifically a green seaweed from shallow water may in fact appear brown. Experts base their classification on more solid ground than colour, using criteria such as structure or life history. Colour gives a rough indication of the depth from which the seaweeds have come, green predominating in the highest levels or shallowest water. The brown seaweeds are from the midtide zone and the red seaweeds occur in the deepest water.

A sponge (unidentified).

Among the seaweeds I found a number of sponges, one a brightly coloured orange, the others much more subdued in shades of brown and grey and much like beach sand. Sponges are mostly unattractive creatures which have apparently been little studied. Their identification is made doubly difficult by the fact that many species have no particular shape and only microscopic examination can accurately determine their identity. Sponges were long a puzzle to early biologists and it was only in the middle of the last century that it was realised that they were members of the animal kingdom, their constituent cells being closely allied to protozoans, the most primitive member of the 'animals'.

Sponges are in fact organisations of single cells, many of them specialised, arranged in a system of canals and chambers which form the body of the sponge. Water enters by minute pores on the outside surface and provides oxygen and nutrients to the cell colony within. The passage of the water through the sponge is facilitated by the tiny waving arms, or flagella, of specialised cells lining the canals. Sea water is expelled out of the large aperture on the surface which is one of the first things noticed about a sponge. What you find on the beach, however, is almost always just the skeleton of the sponge. In most sponges, the structure is made up of tiny spicules of lime or silica which give it a hard abrasive surface. In the case of bath sponges, the skeleton has a fibrous surface called spongin, which provides the flexibility and softness of those now out-of-date aids to washing.

Before leaving Point Addis at about 11.30 am, I had a quick look through the bushland around the car park. A few of the low-growing Messmate trees were in flower – a much less spectacular flower than the Red Ironbarks I had encountered earlier. Some of these trees were weighed down with very prolific growths of the native vine Dodder Laurel. Dodder Laurel is a parasitic plant which has become adapted to a variety of host plants. Although I am not sure why, it tends to proliferate in disturbed areas such as the one where I found it today on the fringes of a car park. Perhaps the additional light afforded by the removal of trees helps it to establish and develop.

Although at first Dodder Laurel grows from a root in the ground, it soon attaches itself to the host plant by means of suckers, and thereafter obtains its nutrients from this new source, its original root system withering away. The plant is entirely adapted to a twining existence, the leaves being reduced to minute scales. The traditional role of the leaf in the assimilation of carbon dioxide has in this plant been almost entirely usurped by the twining mass of green stems. The flowers are small and inconspicuous and only the fruits, which are sometimes bright red, add any obvious colour to this strange plant.

JUNE

LEFT: A new day arrives, Point Addis.

*ABOVE: Leaves of the Scented
Sundew* (Drosera whittakeri)*.*

ABOVE: Split Point lighthouse, Aireys Inlet.

BELOW: The beach northeast of Urquhart Bluff.

8 JUNE

There was no real sunrise this morning because of the ever-present sea mist which is such a feature of this coastline. The sun did not appear in its full glory until after 9 am, and then only intermittently. Nevertheless, I spent a good deal of time photographing the shoreline: a long, curving beach stretching northeast towards Anglesea beneath a bank of threatening backlit clouds.

There were masses of kelp on the beach, washed in by recent storms. This is a fairly regular occurrence here and it says much for the richness of the source of kelp, which presumably lies on the seaward edge of the rocks lining the shore between here and Aireys Inlet, five kilometres to the south. The rate of regrowth to restore these constant losses must be quite formidable. It also makes you wonder about the processes involved in the breakdown of these huge, tough, leathery straps of seaweed which eventually find their way back into the sea on an outgoing tide.

Even before you see it, you become aware of the powerful smell of iodine associated with kelp. Iodine is an element which strangely is essential to certain brown and red seaweeds and yet it is not required by land plants, although its role in the metabolism of seaweeds still remains unclear. Although iodine occurs in minute amounts in sea water (less than one part per 10 million), seaweeds actively accumulate it and iodine harvested from seaweed was once the prime source of this element essential to human beings.

Later this morning on the way to Lorne, I was attracted by the reflections of the Split Point lighthouse at Aireys Inlet in the still water at the mouth

of the Painkalac Creek. It is a most picturesque lighthouse, tall, white and slender with a bright red roof. It was one of the number of lighthouses and signals established at key navigational points along the coastline of southeastern Australia following the building of the Cape Otway lighthouse in 1848.

The formation of the lagoon at Aireys Inlet is unusual and unlike anything else on this coastline. The stream curves round behind a huge sand bar well covered with vegetation, including large examples of the spreading Moonah tea tree, and is well stabilised against wind erosion. Like so many creeks along this coast, the Painkalac often fails in most seasons to reach the sea, its entrance being blocked by a sand bar.

From Aireys Inlet I drove on to the Lorne Forest Park and up Garvey Track which leads ultimately to the highest point in the Otways – Mount Cowley (680 metres). A steep path leads off Garvey Track to the Kalimna Falls and runs down the northern face of a steep valley. The Lower Kalimna Falls are unusual in that the creek flows over a concave rock wall and it is possible to stand behind the falling sheet of water. I did just this to take some photographs, although it will be difficult to reproduce the scene on film. For an overhang such as this to have formed, there must be a great difference in the relative hardness of successive layers of the sedimentary rock.

To reach the Upper Kalimna Falls requires a steady climb and although the walking track is said to be 1.3 kilometres, it seemed much more than that to me. Unlike the Lower Falls, this cascade is well sheltered from sunlight and is also considerably higher, perhaps a 15-metres drop. Today I found it very wet and cold, an almost foreboding atmosphere, and I doubt that the falls themselves see much sunshine except for a few hours on clear days in summer. Everything here was bathed in mist and the huge rocks at the foot of the falls were slimy and treacherous to walk on; the whole scene, with its backdrop of huge tree ferns, has a distinctly primeval look.

Not surprisingly, this permanently wet environment has a very good representation of ground ferns, filmy ferns, water ferns and mosses. High above in full sunlight I could see up into the top of tall Blackwoods and eucalypts. On one tree I noted a clump of Drooping Mistletoe. It was interesting to contrast these two microenvironments covering this one small piece of ground. At my level it was a permanently moist, dark and virtually windless situation, and yet 40 metres above, it was dry, windy and sunlit.

On the way back, I photographed some Coral Fungi that had emerged

ABOVE: Flame Fungus (Clavulinopsis miniata).

RIGHT: Rocky coastline, Aireys Inlet

from the side of the walking track. A red specimen, it looked very much like the Flame Fungus (*Clavulinopsis miniata*) and perhaps the yellow ones growing nearby were merely a colour variant of this same species although there is a closely allied yellow species (*Clavulinopsis amoena*). The red form had a very vivid colour and a shape which to the imaginative observer might conjure up visions of a flame. Like a number of other well-known fungi, including the common mushroom, they have an extraordinarily wide distribution throughout the world. The Flame Fungus has been found in heathland and forest in Victoria, but also appears as far afield as South Africa, Ceylon, Madagascar, Malaysia and Papua New Guinea. Unlike toadstools, which have obvious gills, and Bracket Fungi, which distribute their spores from tiny holes or pores on the undersurface, Coral Fungi spread theirs from the entire surface of the fruiting body and have no specially located structures to contain the spores.

There is much Blanketleaf growing in this valley. It is a striking plant and most aptly named. The long, narrow, lanceolate leaves are dark green on the upper surface and relatively smooth, but the undersurface is white and deeply felted. The plant may grow as high as 10 metres in favourable situations and the small yellow flowers are grouped in relatively inconspicuous clusters. Botanically, Blanketleaf is closely allied to much smaller shrubs of the daisy family (Compositae) like the fireweed that frequently occurs with it along the side of tracks and roads.

I have often wondered why a number of these trees of the dense gullies have a white furry leaf undersurface. As well as Blanketleaf, the most spectacular example, there is Musk Daisy Bush, Hazel Pomaderris and Satinwood. I have read that the felted undersurface protects the leaf against insect attack. However, this seems unlikely since why should such gully plants be any more susceptible to insects, particularly as leaf-eating insects tend to be much commoner and of greater variety in open forest country. Another explanation, which at first seems strange since these plants are found in our heaviest rainfall areas, is that it is a protection against the effects of drought. The fur, or down, covers the stomata, the pores on the lower surface through which the leaves transpire, and would certainly help to reduce water loss. Whilst in most seasons there is abundant rainfall, once in every 50 or 100 years, a major drought will occur and in these circumstances even these sheltered trees become vulnerable and can die. Occurrences of major drought seem rare by the measure of our own lifespan but over the period of several million years during which these trees evolved, these species could well have been subjected to many thousands of such stressful periods. Those individuals with slightly more furry leaves could be favoured and selected out by evolutionary pressure and eventually become dominant.

As is so often the case in these wet sclerophyll rainforests I saw and heard few birds. There were some thornbills, which are always hard to identify because the various species are so alike, but I think they were Buff Rumped Thornbills. I also heard the occasional cry of crows (Australian Ravens).

My luck with birds changed as I drove back to Anglesea. On the way I hastily pulled up to take photographs of a Great Egret, perfectly reflected in the mirrorlike surface of the Erskine River. Browsing among the rushes with the egret were several Masked Plovers and a White-faced Heron. The river today produced a superbly reflective surface for photography.

ABOVE: Wind patterns on a small sand dune, Urquhart Bluff.

BELOW: Great Egret.

It was really an evil sort of ooze, since the egret and the heron were actually able to walk on what appeared in the distance to be water!

The Great Egret, commonly seen along this coastline, is a cosmopolitan bird found on all the continents except Antarctica. I have seen them in many of the estuaries along the seaboard, often near townships, stalking insects and frogs and, on the whole, fairly oblivious to human beings.

17 JUNE

My destination today was Cape Otway and I took the dirt road leading off the Ocean Road to the lighthouse. It was a lot smoother today than in my last visit some months ago. Rain has dampened the corrugations or perhaps they have graded the road. Before reaching the lighthouse I took the Blanket Bay turnoff to the east and finally another track to Parkers Hill above the mouth of the Parker River. The very tiny bay here is less than 100 metres across but behind it has a surprisingly expansive sandy flat described as a tidal delta of in-filled sand.

On the way down to the Parker River I was pleased to locate Ghost Fungus (*Pleurotus nidiformis*) at the base of a Messmate. The luminosity of this toadstool is puzzling. It is so striking on a dark night with its green glowing light, and yet no reason has yet been advanced as to why this fungus should exhibit this strange property. Some other fungi are also

Winter sunrise, Beech Forest.

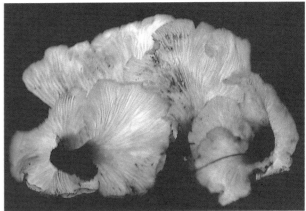

luminous but few, it any, are as spectacular as the Ghost Fungus. Some observers have suggested that the eerie light may attract small night-flying insects which aid in the dissemination of its spores, but this has never been demonstrated. Perhaps the biochemical reaction which leads to this phosphorescence, a process that is known and understood, is merely a part of a chain of processes and the light produced has neither purpose nor meaning in itself.

The rock platforms at Parker River contain some of the most spectacular rock formations I have seen on this coastline and the variety of colour in the rock is very marked indeed, ranging from jade to brown. The sand above the cliffs is breaking away in places and is bound by a blue-leaf daisy, Cushion Bush, and in some places pigface or Karkalla. I photographed a Cushion Bush that was hanging precariously onto a very thin layer of soil which appeared about to peel off and fall on my head! On the western side of the bay, huge rock sculptures in the cliff stand out in spectacular fashion.

I found excellent examples of barnacles and tube worms (Galeolaria) on the flat rock surfaces above where the waves were breaking. These barnacles were dead, with the operculum or trapdoor at the top of the shell missing, leaving a more or less spherical hole. The barnacle is unique among shellfish in its method of feeding. The trapdoor, which actually consists of two doors, opens to release 12 bristle-covered limbs or cirri which, when water covers the barnacles, are released and direct food into the mouth. Unlike other shellfish, they are hermaphroditic but, strangely, introduce

ABOVE LEFT: The Ghost Fungus (Pleurotus nidiformis).

ABOVE: The Ghost Fungus taken by its own light at night (7-hour exposure).

BELOW: Rock formations, Parker River

ABOVE: Tube worms
(Galeolaria caespitosa) and
dead barnacles (unidentified).

RIGHT: Blue periwinkle
(Nodilittorina unifasciata), a
shellfish which spends the greater
part of its life high on the shore
platform and out of the water.

sperm into their neighbouring shells, although self-fertilisation by isolated individuals also occurs. These barnacles were a species of rock barnacle (*Chamaesipho columna*) which is very common along this coastline between mid- and high-tide levels.

There were many small blue periwinkles clustered in groups well above high-tide level where they could seldom expect to be covered by sea water. These small shellfish belong to the family Littorinidae, the true periwinkles. They have attracted worldwide interest because they have adapted, and appear to be continuing to adapt, to a life out of the water. Several species may each occupy different levels on the shore platform. In Victoria *Nodilittorina unifasciata* occupies the highest zone and a closely related species *N preaetermissa* is found in the layer immediately below.

The gills of these sea snails have been found to be somewhat differently structured to other marine molluscs, enabling them to live comfortably in air. The late Edmund Gill once kept two snails of *N unifasciata* alive on his desk without water for a period of two months, demonstrating just how well this mollusc has adapted to a dry life above the normal span of the tides.

I photographed some shell remnants this morning on the floor of a shallow rock cave in the cliffs to the west of the mouth of the Parker River. This cave would have provided shelter for Aboriginal people from the rain but not from the southwest winds and may have been used only in favourable weather. Densely packed small shells, mostly limpets and mussels, were embedded in 30 centimetres of black soil on the floor of the cave, all surprisingly well preserved.

During the early 1960s much larger shell deposits in the base of two rock shelters about three kilometres upstream from the mouth of the nearby Aire River were examined by a team of anthropologists. Using carbon dating they estimated that the shelters may have been used for a period of up to 600 years. Remnants were found of most species of the common shellfish that occur here today and also bones of animals, fish and seals.

Analysis of the artefacts found at these shelters suggests that their use may have changed over time. At first they may have been used as camps in the summer months. Later they may have become sites for the production of bone points, an activity likely to have been pursued in the cooler months of the year.

Bone implements are believed to have played an important role in the manufacture of the animal-skin cloaks characteristic of the tribes of this region. Anyone familiar with the cold winds that blow remorselessly across the coast and plains of southwest Victoria can readily appreciate the need for such warm clothing. Bone pegs were also used to spread and dry skins, and bone was fashioned into sharp needles to sew individual skins of possums and koalas together and also to provide a means of fastening the garments when worn. Bone awls were used to cut the ornamentation displayed on the inside of the cloaks. Bone was also employed to tip wooden spears which in the Otways were claimed to have been made from Satinwood – the bandid spears – or lighter spears from grass tree stems.

Because of the paucity of records made at the time of European contact and the fact that they died out so quickly, very little is known about the culture of the Aborigines of the Otways and much has been left to conjecture. It is believed, however, that one tribe occupied the Otway Range and its immediate surroundings, including Cape Otway. These people spoke the Gadubanud dialect, a word meaning 'King Parrot speakers'.

The territory of Gadubanud has been defined as being bordered in the west by the Gellibrand River, in the northwest by the Barwon River between the present-day towns of Forrest and Birregurra, and in the north by a line between Birregurra and Aireys Inlet, the ocean forming the eastern and southern boundaries. Five clans have been recorded, though there may well have been more. Estimates of the population of the Gadubanud vary widely but at the time of European settlement they may have numbered two to three hundred.

How the Gadubanud occupied their tribal lands remains very speculative. Whether they roamed widely, utilising the coastal resources on a transient, seasonal basis and retreating far inland to the northern edges of the ranges during the colder months, or whether there were more or less permanent coastal population centres, perhaps based on resource-rich sheltered valleys such as those of the Aire and Johanna rivers, are questions at the centre of this debate. The weight of evidence suggests the dense inland forests of the Otways were not inhabited on a regular basis but were visited,

ABOVE: *An Aboriginal midden.*

BELOW: *Late winter afternoon haze over Station Beach.*

Sunlight on fast-flowing water produces the stunning multicoloured effect of the Rainbow Falls.

presumably to gather vegetable food, such as the pith of the ferns, or Satinwood for spear shafts, or Austral Mulberry used for firesticks.

Later in the afternoon I walked from the northwest side of the lighthouse to Station Beach immediately west of the lighthouse. This last section of the track is very rough but it finally leads to the beach and a nearby rocky shore platform. Here I spent time photographing the huge waves smashing into the rocks and the Rainbow Falls a further 600 metres to the east.

I had assumed that the Rainbow Falls got their name from the rainbow pattern formed by sunlight on the fast-flowing water, but it could also be attributed to the multitude of coloured bands on the cliffs over which they run. The immediate area of the falls is almost jet-black but on either side there are successive vertical bands of various colours – red-brown, ochre, orange and yellow – and the first impression you have is that this is a scene from the Northern Territory rather than one from the southern coast of the continent. In geomorphological terms, this feature is classed as a tufa wall. It is made up of calc tufa, a deposit of calcium carbonate like those found in caves as stalactites and stalagmites. Springs in the dune limestone above the cliffs are rich in calcium bicarbonate which has been deposited as calc tufa where the falls emerge at the cliff face over the underlying Cretaceous rocks.

Beyond Rainbow Falls, Point Flinders juts out sharply into Bass Strait and below, on the shoreline rocks, a group of Great Cormorants was gathered. In the distance they looked like an assemblage of rock fishermen.

23&24 JUNE

The Otway Ridge is a picture at the moment. Even in driving rain the lush green winter grass stands out and everywhere there is very good winter paddock feed available despite the recent heavy rainfalls. The country looks in great heart and I saw several paddocks heavily stocked with ewes and lambs.

At Moonlight Head I made an effort to photograph the boiling sea from the top of the Gable. It was blowing a gale and with the driving rain it made photography extremely difficult. Water droplets were accumulating on the lens and I quickly retreated to the shelter of the she-oak grove behind the cliff edge. The protection afforded by these close-growing trees

A wet winter morning in pasturelands on the Otway Ridge.

Stormy seas at Moonlight Head.

is quite remarkable. The wind at the cliff face created a constant roar and had the top of the she-oaks sighing in response, but beneath this tightknit grove it was surprisingly calm and dry. Even in today's dreadful conditions it would make a surprisingly snug camp site just a few metres in from the roaring gale at the clifftop. Not surprisingly there was no bird, animal or insect life to be seen, but I did find a few toadstools. I noted a rare bright pink species (*Cantharellus lilacinus*) with exposed gills and a trumpetlike shape which made an interesting photographic study.

I imagine that temperatures here, even in the depths of winter, would remain above freezing and there would be few, if any, frosts so that the fruiting bodies of the toadstool and other types of fungi growing here survive for longer than they would in the forests further inland.

The next morning I again visited Moonlight Head, this time in better weather. The track to the head leads across some paddocks and eventually ends near a set of stockyards on an exposed knoll high above Bass Strait. To the east it overlooks the huge landslip between Moonlight Head and Point Reginald. I left my car on the top of a hill and walked down the last section because I reckoned it was too risky to take the car any further down the track as I might not have been able to get back.

The walk was very enjoyable in the winter sunshine. Along the track, excellent protection was afforded by a surprisingly dense and tall stand of Messmate, perhaps 10 metres high, on the lower-lying sections of the track. I saw two wallabies, the first a young Redneck and the other, a more mature Scrub Wallaby. The latter, as is so often the case, did not notice me until I was almost upon it and then it made off in a great panic. Both animals had been attracted to the closely cropped regrowth along the track, which is presumably kept that way as a fire break. Wattle Matrush and Common Heath were very prominent in this mown vegetation and the grasses would provide feed for the wallabies.

Beyond the stockyards the walk down to the beach at Moonlight Head was very easy going through pleasant undulating pasture. I paused to photograph some very contented Jersey cows grazing above the wild seas with huge and grim looking cliffs of the Gable in the background. Somehow it appealed to me as a strange contrast.

At one point I disturbed a very large flock of magpies, perhaps 30 in all. You seldom see more than a few of these birds together and I wondered what set of circumstances would cause them to congregate.

Above a small beach immediately west of Moonlight Head I virtually had to slide down the last few metres at a point where the track peters out and drops onto a small, sheltered patch of sand. Here lie the remnants of a barge which broke away while being towed from Adelaide to Geelong in 1935 and for years could be seen from the top of the Gable. Now it is broken up and the rusted pieces of the engine and superstructure are scattered over the rocks and embedded in the sand in strange, surrealistic shapes, alternately exposed and flooded by the surging waves.

The walk back to the car was steep but easy enough and I thought of how much more difficult travel must have been before this country was cleared and how the famous 'Chinese' Morrison, then a seventeen-year-old schoolboy from Geelong College, had walked this same coastline in the summer of 1880, covering the 1,210 kilometres from Queenscliff to Adelaide in 46 days. This particular section of the southwest coast is extremely rugged and dissected, and even now is covered in places with thick impenetrable scrub interspersed with sections of huge, sometimes nearly vertical, cliffs.

Morrison, who must surely rate as one of the most extraordinary people produced by this country, was also the first person to travel the Murray River, from Wodonga to Lake Alexandrina, in a small boat a distance of 2,496 kilometres and which he achieved solo the next year. His most memorable achievement of endurance, however, was to cover what the ill-fated Burke and Wills expedition tried to do, but alone and in the reverse direction. Morrison was highly sceptical of that disastrous and much publicised venture and was convinced he could achieve the feat on his own, with no horses, camels or guides. He covered the 3,299 kilometres from Normanton in the Gulf of Carpentaria to Deniliquin in 123 days, but received very little publicity for his epic feat. Later he was to earn world fame as the Peking correspondent of the London *Times*, and later as political adviser to Yuan Shih-kai, the first President of the Chinese Republic.

In this particular section of his coastal journey, Morrison set off from

ABOVE: *Toadstool* (Cantharellus lilacinus).

BELOW: *A Scrub Wallaby above Moonlight Beach.*

Remnants of a wrecked barge,
Moonlight Head.

Glenaire at 7.30 am on 6 January and reached the Gellibrand River 10 hours later. Fortunately, he followed a narrow track inland from the coast which must have taken him up to the Otway Ridge, somewhere south of the present town of Lavers Hill, and down the spur to the vicinity of the Gable. In doing this and avoiding the treacherous coastline, Morrison probably heeded a cryptic telegraph message he received from his friend Stewart MacArthur while at Apollo Bay. MacArthur, whose father was part-owner of Glenample Station at Princetown, warned of the impassable nature of the coast and told him to head inland between Cape Otway and Princetown. Being Morrison, he would undoubtedly have survived had he attempted to follow the cliffs, but he would have spent a much longer time reaching the relative safety of the Gellibrand River.

28 JUNE

My destination today was Moonlight Beach. As dawn broke I stopped at various points along the road to take photographs of the rising mist. One interesting light effect was that of the first rays of sunshine playing on an old broken trunk of Mountain Ash near Weeaproinah. I have photographed it before but since that time it has been further damaged in a wind storm leaving only a butt perhaps 10 metres high.

At Moonlight Beach the weather was very uninviting: constant drizzle and a strong cold onshore wind. The track down to the beach was wet and slippery and I took a good deal of time to negotiate it, slipping and sliding all the while. On the way down it was easy to see an offshore reef, part of which is a large flat rock platform further out to sea and which was taking a powerful beating by the waves this morning.

The creeks running into the sea here form what could be classed as hanging valleys. These occur along the coastline where waves erode away the cliff face faster than the stream develops its gully. They drop suddenly over the last few metres to the beach like small waterfalls. They are minute streams with little more than a trickle of water. In other steeper places, water drops directly down the cliff face onto the beach seemingly at random and from no clear-cut surface streams.

Hoping to locate the graves of those who lost their lives in the wreck of the *Fiji* in 1891, I made my way up the western bank of Wreck Creek. At first this was a matter of carefully negotiating a very steep rocky stream with one or two treacherous and slimy sections, but eventually I had to venture into the thick tea tree scrub on the western side of the valley. I climbed towards the top of the hill but the undergrowth eventually proved to be virtually impenetrable and I reluctantly made my way back to the beach.

Eleven members of the *Fiji* were drowned attempting to reach shore. A young settler, Arthur Wilkinson, who had been alerted to the disaster by the chance discovery of an exhausted survivor, heroically swam out to save the ship's carpenter. He finally managed to get him back to the ship but was himself struck by the anchor chain in the pounding surf and died aboard the grounded ship. History has it that much looting took place and there were stories of caches of whisky and other contraband that were

ABOVE: An old tree trunk in the mist at Weeaproinah.

BELOW: A swift moth that flies in midwinter (Oxycanus antipoda, previously fuscomaculatus).

*RIGHT: Short-stalked barnacles
(Lepas anserifera).*

*BELOW: The Fly Agaric
(Amanita muscaria).*

buried and available in the district long afterwards. Two of the drowned crew are buried above Wreck Beach. I recall seeing the graves many years ago but couldn't find the site today, perhaps because it has become overgrown in the absence of fires.

On the way back to the foot of the Racecourse Steps I found a piece of driftwood covered with goose barnacles, all still very much alive. This species was probably the Short-stalked Barnacle which, like other kinds of goose barnacles, are creatures of open water attaching themselves to floating objects. Once washed up on the beach, however, they soon die. Although very different in appearance to rock barnacles, goose barnacles have similar limbs, or cirri, which they extend to capture their prey. Although I am not sure that it would save them for long, I threw the driftwood back into the sea and watched the goose barnacles on the surface of the beam unfold their cirri as if in appreciation of their return to their natural watery environment.

After lunch I made my way to the Beauchamp Falls. Although I had been to these falls recently I wanted to revisit the area to obtain some shots of the Aire River where it flows through a stand of Myrtle Beech and tree ferns.

ABOVE LEFT: *Fungus growing on fallen branch* (Heterotextus pezizaeformis).

ABOVE: *The Velvet Foot* (Collybia flammulina).

For this time of the year there was a surprisingly large number of toadstools about, particularly the spectacular Fly Agaric. Many of these were orange rather than the usual bright red, and few had strong development of the characteristic white, mealy pustules on their caps. There were a number of other toadstools growing with them which I could not identify but one that I could: the Ghost Fungus (*Pleurotus nidiformis*).

The Fly Agaric (*Amanita muscaria*) is perhaps the most spectacular and best known toadstool in the world. It has been a part of history, appearing in paintings from medieval France and in murals from Greek and Roman times. The brilliant red cap, white spots and white stem attract immediate attention even from those who would not notice any other form of toadstool. Its fame is also associated with its toxicity which for centuries has been exploited to kill or stupefy flies by adding pieces of the toadstool to milk or to solutions of sugar and water placed in situations visited by flies. The poisonous properties of the toadstool seem to be principally located in the skin. With special treatment prior to cooking, however, the Fly Agaric can be eaten with safety.

The Fly Agaric is certainly not as dangerous as the closely related Death Cap (*Amanita phalloides*) found in Europe. This highly poisonous toadstool has claimed many lives over the years. Very recently the Death Cap was recorded in Melbourne growing under oak trees and perhaps along with the Fly Agaric it came in soil surrounding imported seedlings years ago. The fact that the fruiting body, the toadstool, has only just now been observed does not rule out the possibility that the fungus has been in Australia for a long time. The mycelium or the vegetative stage of the fungus could have existed in soil around the roots of oak trees for years and the occasional production of the toadstools, which have an undistinguished light olive-green colour, would be unlikely to have attracted attention. Unfortunately the Death Cap was identified here after someone was accidentally poisoned as a result of eating it. The untreated flesh of the Fly Agaric while not fatal does cause intoxication in small quantities and serious illness in larger doses. The intoxicating properties were widely recognised by several races and the Inuits (Eskimos) of northwest America and the Vikings of Scandinavia both made use of it as a part of feasts and ceremonies.

The Fly Agaric is an obligate associate of pines, Silver Birches and chestnuts and is found only around these trees where the mycorrhiza and the roots of the trees live in partnership.

JULY

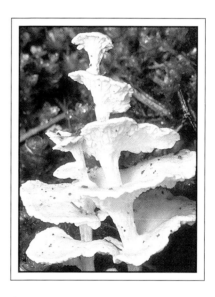

LEFT: *Aire River in full flood below*
Hopetoun Falls.

ABOVE: An unusual tiered fungus
(Podoserpula pusio).

8 & 9 JULY

There is a well-marked but very narrow track along the East Barwon River which leads to Lake Elizabeth. The valley here is surprisingly open with a few tall blue gums, Hazel Pomaderris and an understorey of grasses, mainly Tassock Grass (*Poa* sp). The massive surge of water which occurred after the formation of Lake Elizabeth swept away the original vegetation and at the same time cut a straighter course in the previously winding alignment of the East Barwon. The lake itself is difficult to survey because of the heavy growth of rushes at the water's edge and shrub growth around the foreshore. However, I did manage a few photographs showing the old,

Lichen-covered trunks of Silver Wattles (Acacia dealbata)

*Fossil leaves attributed to a long-extinct relation of the Austral King Fern (*Todea barbara*) which grows nearby.*

dead trees which have somehow managed to remain standing in the water for over 30 years.

Lake Elizabeth was formed in June 1952 after a period of unprecedented rainfall. In nearby Tanbryn half a metre of rain fell in a few days. A huge landslip occurred during the night and created a dam wall that impounded water which eventually reached back one and a half kilometres to the east. However, on 19 August of the following year, after another burst of heavy rain, the river cut through the dam bank which was reduced in height by no less than 26 metres. The consequent huge surge of water carried boulders and debris down the East Barwon and must have come as a tremendous surprise to the landholders further downriver. The lake was reduced to a fifth of its original size but it has retained this area since that day.

I stayed overnight at Lavers Hill and the wind blew noisily all night on this very exposed part of the Otway Ridge. The forecast was considerably worse than the earlier prediction and they were now saying that there would be gales from the northwest with showers, and there was a graziers' alert out as well. Nevertheless, I decided to stick to my original plan and to visit the coast below the Rivernook Track near Moonlight Beach. As it turned out, the weather remained dry and, in fact, in the shelter of this

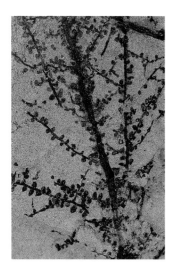

ABOVE: *Fine rootlets of a fossil conifer show the nodules formed by fungi (Mycorrhiza).*

BELOW: *A pebble beach near Moonlight Beach.*

very steep-walled bay, it was surprisingly calm and the sun even came out later in the morning. The seas, however, were very wild. An occasional big wave sent foam surging up the beach to where I was searching for fossils in the cliff face.

I located some fossils in a bed of siltstone above the beach. The rock was curiously soft and grey-green and the fossil fragments showed as dark markings with some recognisable leaf shapes. They were the leaves of nonflowering plants, mainly ferns, the remnants of which are believed to have been deposited on flood plains and preserved in a poorly drained anaerobic environment. I was fascinated by the detail preserved in the tiny fragments of once delicate plants. Even the smallest veins and indentations in the pinnae of the ferns could be clearly seen with the naked eye.

In these same deposits, fossilised tree roots with root nodules still attached have been found. These have been attributed to a conifer tree distantly related to the Mountain Plum Pine of alpine Victoria. The fossil roots and the roots of Mountain Plum Pine both have similarly shaped nodules which are formed by a mutually beneficial association between the tree and a type of fungus; this association is called mycorrhiza. Research on the function of mycorrhizae has shown that they enhance the uptake of phosphate and to a lesser extent nitrogen by the host plant. For its part, the fungus receives a reward of carbohydrate provided by the plant.

It does seem extraordinary that such a complex and intricate relationship and one we are still learning about today was operating 100 million years ago. These fossil roots also provided clues about the nature of the country in which the trees grew. Unlike the soils containing the beautifully preserved leaves, which must have been ill drained, mycorrhizae would only function efficiently in well-aerated soil and only flourish in a situation of low fertility where their activity would be essential to the wellbeing of the host trees. So scientists hypothesise that such free draining, low nutrient soils occurred on levees formed alongside a river meandering across a flood plain.

LEFT: *Rolling pebbles, washed by waves, Moonlight Beach.*

ABOVE: *Tektite, Rivernook Track.*
(Top): Front surface.
(Bottom): Rear surface.

There were many coloured pebbles and small boulders on the beach, including agate. There was also much red jasper. The origin of these two semiprecious stones along the coastline has always been somewhat of a puzzle. There is evidence that there is a not-too-distant submerged outcrop of Later Palaeozoic sediments from which the rocks have been dislodged by the action of the sea. Divers have reported pebble beds in several fathoms of water directly out from the shore.

One might also ask why the grains of sand among the pebbles do not also have the same smooth, rounded shape. The answer to this lies in the protection afforded to these small stones or grains of sand by a layer of water which surrounds them and prevents them being smoothed and rounded.

On my way back to the car which I left in the vicinity of Moonlight Beach I looked for tektites, sometimes called Australites. These strange glasslike objects made of silica and believed to have fallen from space were once common in this area. Tektites are found in many parts of the world, including several parts of Australia. The Port Campbell–Moonlight Head 'strewn field' has been the source of thousands of specimens.

Areas where the vegetation has been removed, such as this dirt road, the Rivernook Track, have been a rich source of tektites. They very frequently have symmetrical shapes, and here they usually look like buttons one to two centimetres in diameter and appear black, although if held up to the light they are partially translucent. The search for tektites can be fascinating;

some days may be fruitful but weeks may pass without further success.

The anterior or front end of tektites is often characterised by striations said to have been formed as they entered the earth's atmosphere. One theory is that they are remnants of debris thrown up after a meteor struck the moon. Another is that they have been 'fired' at the earth by a volcano on the moon.

Because tektites here have mostly been found on the surface of man-made structures, particularly roads and borrow pits, it has been suggested that they may have fallen since the time of European settlement. The fact that the finds are restricted to these exposed sites, however, seems much more likely to be due to them having been covered elsewhere by soil and hence not visible. Their characteristic shapes, chemical composition and the very limited area of the fall, strongly indicates that these tektites arrived in a single shower in prehistoric times.

14 JULY

I left Melbourne at 6.50 am and arrived at Bells Beach an hour and a half later. The weather was dull, but the forecast was for fine weather. I walked along to the Jarosite Headland, southwest of Bells Headland. There is much yellow colour in the cliffs and multicoloured rocks are strewn in piles along the beach. An old jetty, or the remains thereof, is nestled in against the low cliffs at the eastern end of the beach. Perhaps eight stumps, silvered with age and streaked with growths of red-brown lichen, are all that is left of it now.

I photographed whirling patterns formed by the grains of black rutile on the sand. An oxide of the metal titanium, rutile is heavier than the quartz grains of sand and is separated out from the mass of sand by the receding tidal water, much as gold remains at the rear of the panning vessel.

The cliffs rise steadily in height as you move west towards the Jarosite Headland. Originally they would have been of similar stature to the headland itself but a huge landslip between Bells and Jarosite Headland has formed an amphitheatre covering several hectares now densely wooded with Moonah and other coastal plants. The leading edge of this huge slumped mass of rock and earth now forms the much lower cliffs of the eastern section of the bay.

The lower layers of the cliffs closer to the headland have a black, almost purple look about them. Yet they do not strike you as being so dark when viewed at a distance, for instance from Bells Headland. The jarosite, a strange yellow colour, is confined to a layer several metres thick in the uppermost sediments of this bluff.

Jarosite Headland itself is a huge cliff with piles of fallen rocks and rubble on the beach at its base. The undercutting action of the waves seems concentrated on this prominence. In places the tops of the cliffs jut out metres over the beach below and make you very wary of walking too close, in case you become a victim to one of the rockfalls which continually occur.

On my return to the car park at Bells I detoured off the walking track which winds up the cliff, to examine the rugged limestone profile of the headland. There were rich deposits of fossil here confined to quite discrete layers in the profile. I took a photograph of fragments of fossils which

Patterns formed by minerals in the beach sand.

looked much like pieces of present-day sea urchins. These layers of sedimentary limestone were laid down under the sea in the late Oligocene period over 20 million years ago.

Later, walking up the path, I watched the graceful sweeping flight of a Whistling Kite, which we used to call Whistling Eagles. It was a very pale specimen but readily identified by its size, flight and by the characteristic markings on the underwings. The kite was catching updraughts of air at the edge of the cliffs and soaring effortlessly out over the amphitheatre of windswept bushland below. These birds are primarily carrion feeders but also prey on small animals, insects and reptiles. I would imagine that the interface of bushland and cleared pasture land near the edge of the cliffs would provide a good hunting ground of rabbits who eat the pasture and shelter in scrub on the margins.

Later I was diverted by the noisy calls of a White-naped Honeyeater

which took up temporary residence in the Messmate above my head. They are a striking bird with olive and green plumage and with a pronounced white mark on the head. Although a honeyeater and therefore partial to nectar, they also feed on insects. Nectar is their major source of energy but it does not meet their need for protein. They must seek out insects to supplement the nutriment they obtain from flowers.

It has been suggested that the plants and the birds that frequent areas of low nutrient soils such as these have coevolved to provide a system which is to their mutual advantage. The insect population is not high and so birds, in the absence of nectar, would have to work very hard to meet their dietary needs for energy and protein by catching them. The proliferation of nectar-producing plants so characteristic of these impoverished soils has been matched by a parallel development of birds and mammals (mainly possums) specially able to utilise the nectar provided by the flowers. The birds and animals have gained by having a source of energy to help them catch insects and the plants by the increasing number of vectors available to pollinate their flowers and to favour outcrossing.

This afternoon I spent exploring the valley of the lower stretches of the Cumberland River. The Cumberland is one of the biggest of the several streams which flow southeast from the crest of the Otway Range to the sea. I approached the river walk from the camping ground near the mouth, just off the Ocean Road about 15 kilometres south of Lorne.

I found some very beautiful stretches along the lower river as I strolled slowly along. The stream alternates between rapids with many exposed rocks, rounded boulders and angular lichen-covered stones, and smaller ponded sections where the surface of the water remains unruffled. The still sections beautifully reflected the arching and cream-trunked Manna Gums and olive-green Blackwoods along the banks.

Dancing Trees—Manna Gums (Eucalyptus viminalis) *on the Lower Cumberland River.*

There are a variety of trees and shrubs in this steep-sided valley and I noted Hazel Pomaderris, the Prickly Currantbush (a most unlikely looking cousin of the Looking Glass Plant), Southern Blue Gums, Messmate and Musk Daisy Bush. The latter derives its name from the musk odour of the timber and is sometimes used as a source of furniture wood because of its beautifully figured grain.

I was impressed by the great diversity of scenery of the lower Cumberland. The sheltered and dense forested country along the river contrasts with the huge craggy cliffs above. They rear up in places 100 metres or so almost sheer above the river. The windswept vegetation on the top is exposed to the full force of the southerly winds. There are cliff sections where the normally grey coloured rocks have been weathered to a red-brown colour. It reminded me of a central Australian scene with a foreground of white-trunked Mannas which might well have been the Ghost Gums which so often adorn photographs and paintings of the red centre.

I was interested to note the honeycomb weathering on the face of these

Distant view of Point Roadknight from above Urquhart Bluff.

Cretaceous rock walls at a height many metres above the river. This would suggest that despite the belief that honeycomb weathering, on the coast anyway, is mainly produced by wave splash, it must also have other causes such as the action of rain or wind. There is certainly no saltwater here.

I spent some time photographing a small cascade above Jebbs Pool. Here the river falls suddenly over a bare band of resistant rock about three metres high. This substantial pool has been hollowed out by the swirling water and is used as a source of water for the camping ground a kilometre or more downstream. The band of rock forming the ridge over which the stream falls contains some large spherical potholes gouged out in a line across the direction of the current of the river. These potholes could only be active when the river is in flood and today the level of the stream is a metre or so below the surface of the rock layer containing them.

At Jebbs Pool I disturbed what I took to have been a stonefly. But I was unable to follow its flight and lost it in a dense patch of Bayonet Grass and water fern. Stoneflies are unusual among insects in that they have no strong seasonal preference for flying and reproducing. Different species can be seen at all times of the year. It is significant that this was the only insect I recall seeing all day, although I have no doubt I could have turned up beetles and other hibernating insects under bark and stones had I cared to look.

I was interested to see that many of the tall trees about Jebbs Pool, which are mainly Manna Gums, are infested with mistletoe. I saw no evidence of it lower down the river and wonder what fortuitous circumstances favour mistletoe's spread up here. The proliferation of mistletoe is attributed to the activity of the mistletoe bird which spreads the seed of this parasitic plant on the host trees, usually eucalypts.

I left for home at 3.45 pm with the weather looking distinctly unpromising, but it had held up all day so I couldn't complain!

22 & 23 JULY

I spent the morning at Anglesea, looking for the Brown Cones Fungus, a strange cylindrical fungus about six centimetres high. It is often solitary but sometimes occurs in groups. It was discovered some 20 years ago by an old friend of mine, the late Gordon Beaton. It was called after him: *Underwoodia beatonii*. As the quaint generic name seems to suggest, it grows under trees, specifically Moonahs. It is unusual for a fungus in that it emerges very late in July when most other fungi are finished. It forms part of a dwarf understorey including liverworts, mosses and small flowering plants such as Dwarf Skullcap. Also in abundance today were large colonies of slime fungus.

There was a spectacular show of Common Heath on the heathland. Most of it pink, some red and a small amount white. The variation of colour of Common Heath is intriguing, particularly as some populations are made up wholly of the one colour. Research has revealed that single colour, or monomorphic, populations demonstrate a relationship between colour of the corolla (the tube formed by the united petals) and its length and the colour of the anthers. Colour is apparently an indicator of racial differences within the species.

Among the monomorphic population, a scarlet form found in eastern

Common Heath (Epacris impressa).

A spectacular show of Common Heath.

Victoria and the pink form have long corollas, whereas the white form has a short corolla. Where these different forms grow in the one district, the white population which favours open country flowers in the spring, whereas the pink form found in more shaded situations reaches its peak flowering in winter.

Red is a colour favoured by birds, and honeyeaters have been observed visiting scarlet flowers. The long corolla of this form seems well suited to bird pollination, ensuring that some of the pollen attaches itself to the beak of the visitor. White, on the other hand, is a colour favoured by bees and other insects and the later time of flowering suits insect flower visitors which are absent in the winter months and are better suited to gathering nectar and pollen from short flowers.

The polymorphic populations with variable colour forms exhibit no difference between the lengths of pink and white corollas and it is possible that they are hybrid populations derived from crossing between the single colour forms. To what extent they depend on either insects or birds as vectors to distribute their pollen is a subject for further research.

Later I visited a patch of wildflowers inland from Aireys Inlet. This was one of the areas worst affected by the 1983 fire. At the time there was nothing left except bare ground. Nevertheless, many of the wildflowers have now returned. One of these is the rare Twisted Sun Orchid. This small plant, as its title indicates, has a coiled stem. I found a solitary specimen. The flowering stalk still in bud was threaded through the spiral leaves in a strange fashion. This is one of the earliest sun orchids to flower. It must experience very few days in late August and early September when temperatures are high enough to allow the flower to open. The flower is deep purple in colour and, because of its beauty and rarity, is widely sought after by naturalists and flower photographers.

I also located some patches of the Tiny Helmet Orchid. They are minute and barely visible among the surrounding dead leaves and dwarf plants. Yet when looked at close up, they are very neatly constructed and bright mauve in colour.

In the early afternoon I drove to Cape Volney beyond Cape Otway. I had hoped to climb the cliffs down to the boulder beach and look for fossils. However, I mistook the gully and instead came out between Cape Volney and Point Bowker. Like all this coastal country, it is very scrubby, made up largely of Prickly Moses, tussock grass and Prickly Tea Tree. Fortunately, here there was a track down to the beach. It is an area that cray fishermen use and there were a few lobster pots to be found up in the scrub above the small beach.

There is a large cave here on the eastern or sheltered side of this unnamed point between Cape Volney and Point Bowker. It is a quite substantial overhang and it was obvious that it has been the refuge for quite a number of animals and I could see the clearly marked footprints of foxes. It was also once used by Aborigines because there is an extensive deposit of shells high above the level of the sea. You could see how it would have been ideal for the Aborigines – it is very well sheltered from the west and the southwest, the direction of most of the cold winds.

The beach was littered with much driftwood and beyond the sand to the east there is an extensive boulder beach. The western side of this small bay is characterised by a very extensive rock platform. This is rather lower

ABOVE: *The Tiny Helmet Orchid (*Corybas unguiculatus*).*

BOTTOM LEFT: *A red form of Common Heath (*Epacris impressa*).*

BOTTOM RIGHT: *Winter toadstool (*Laccaria *sp) among the heath.*

131

Cave near Cape Volney.

than other rock platforms and as a result is constantly engulfed by surging waves.

I could find no fossils and few stones on the boulder beach. However, there were some intricate rock patterns in some very large rocks and I took photographs of these.

I wended my way back slowly up the very steep slope and noticed the pastures. They are very low at this time of the year and eaten down to a few centimetres by sheep and rabbits. Nevertheless, there were some very healthy lambs about.

I stayed overnight at Lavers Hill and left early in the morning for Princetown. I wanted to look for fossils in the lower part of the cliffs, midway between Princetown and Port Campbell. I eventually located an area which contained some. At first they are not easy to see, but if you concentrate closely on small sections, all of a sudden you notice tiny shells, quite beautifully preserved. Several of them were very similar to shells we find today, although they are several million years old. They are much more recent, however, than the plant fossils I found recently near Moonlight Beach, which date back over 100 million years. These fossil shells are from the Miocene period and thus would be expected to resemble more closely shells we find today.

There is excellent shelter here in the dunes and there is a prolific growth of several native species, including Seaberry Saltbush, Coast Daisy Bush and Cushion Bush. I also noticed a large specimen of African Boxthorn. It is remarkable how this weed species finds its way along pathways into quite dense native scrub.

On the other side of the dunes towards the Ocean Road, there were some excellent sheep to be seen. The ewes had recently given birth to lambs. Many of them had twins. This is always the sign of a high lambing percentage and usually good husbandry. Along the coast the winters are always warm. They are free of frost although there was a light one today. But the most important thing for sheep here is that the valleys in the dunes

Fossil shell (sassia sp) from Miocene period.

provide excellent shelter against the strong winds.

I returned later in the morning to the coast near Cape Volney and walked down an extremely steep and very scrubby spur. However, the going was so tough with a heavy pack that I had to give up about one-third of the way down. From my final vantage point, I could see many boulders on the shoreline, among which have been found examples of fossilised wood. There was a conifer forest here 100 million years ago in the Cretaceous period. The fossilised stumps, gouged out of the cliff's face by erosion, have fallen down into the sea and finally been thrown up smooth and water-worn on the shore.

The scene must have been very different then, the sea being far to the south with the Antarctic continent perhaps 100 kilometres distant across shallow waters. There were no eucalypts, wattles, tea trees or heaths. Instead it was a very green world dominated by conifers probably looking very much like today's Norfolk Island Pines, and cycads perhaps reminiscent of grass trees, and there were many ferns and mosses. And yet, fossil pollen assemblages and recently discovered fossil plants in closely similar sediments at Koonwarra, south Gippsland, 200 kilometres east of here, indicate there were also some flowering plants. Not flowering trees like magnolias which palaeontologists have searched for in vain for years, but rather inconspicuous herbs, soft and weedlike.

28 JULY

I left home at 4.40 am with an overcast sky and no stars shining but with a generally fine forecast. Fast-moving dark clouds crossed the almost full moon, providing a very dramatic scene on the way down to Port Campbell. The trip was quite uneventful but I noticed yet again the few residual and lonely patches of native scrub along the road as dawn broke. The clearing of the Heytesbury Forest after the Second World War was carried out in a very ruthless manner and very little of the original vegetation remains

133

Lichen (Usnea sp) and moss, Aire River.

today. Some of these patches are along the roadside. There are no trees, but shrubs such as tea trees, wattles and sedges have held out reasonably successfully against the invasion of weeds and the regular pruning onslaught carried out by the local council.

The last few kilometres down to the ocean covers very pleasant landscapes reminiscent of the English Downs, completely cleared but with soft restful contours. It is very green, even lush, for this time of the year. No doubt this reflects the present general weather pattern in Victoria. So far, this winter has been extraordinarily mild with an absence of the frosts inland from the coast which normally inhibit winter growth.

I noticed again how very dense is the cover of Cushion Bush and Blue Tussock Grass binding the rounded caps of the cliffs. In places where they are less than vertical, it provides a soft blue-green vegetative cover for many metres below. On the clifftops much taller bushes of Coast Daisy Bush grow at intervals; they are also basically blue-green but with newer foliage providing a brighter green.

My second destination this morning was the mouth of the Sherbrook River. Here the characteristic high sea cliffs virtually disappear, receding to a few metres in height on the eastern side of the river, and are replaced by a jumbled and eroded mass of dunes on the western bank. A wide, wet sand flat runs westerly and at low tide today yielded some interesting reflections of sky and cloud and a close-up view of the heavy seas, which until then I had only braved from the relative safety of the 40-metre cliffs.

Photography in these locations can be quite hazardous and I was doused twice; once when I slipped on the treacherous algae-covered rocks on the eastern bank of the river, falling flat on my back; and the second time when an unexpected wave caught me as I had my back to the sea. Thankfully, in each case, I was able to avoid wetting the cameras.

I was interested to watch the battle between the incoming waves and the water flowing out from the Sherbrook River. Every half minute or so the waves would race up the beach and a surge of water would spear up the narrow river for perhaps 50 metres, to be quickly replaced by the opposing and swiftly running water from the river.

As I walked back up the steep path to the car I was distracted by very noisy calls of a New Holland Honeyeater which perched about 40 metres away on a correa bush. The correas here with their pale yellow-green flower are among the very few plants to bloom at this time of the year and the honeyeaters would be obtaining nectar from them. The distribution of the varieties of this species (*Correa reflexa*) are puzzling in that the yellow-green form occurs here; the red and green form at Anglesea on the eastern edge of the Otways and at the Parker River; and midway between these two sites, a distinct subspecies (*Correa reflexa* var *nummarifolia*) makes its only appearance on the Australian mainland.

I drove to Beauchamp Falls Reserve where the dark forest floor below the closely planted rows of Douglas Firs is covered with small green twigs and branchlets. Were these blown off by the recent storms or are they a result of possums? There was some evidence of this damage on my previous visit earlier this month but now the ground is quite densely covered with newly dropped needles.

The other marked difference is the almost total absence of toadstools. Not one specimen of the Fly Agaric did I see, or the Ghost Fungus. Just a single group of pinkish-white toadstools with which I am not familiar. The cooler July weather has obviously killed them off and it was noticeable how much colder it is now beneath this very dark tree canopy than, say, under the Mountain Ash forest and the rainforest along the Aire River next door. Despite this, it must be said that to have such a profusion of toadstools in early June as I saw on my last visit is unusual and in a normal winter I believe there would be few to be seen after the end of May.

The recent wind storms obviously found their way into the upper reaches

The moon rises into an early evening sky.

of the Aire and several large branches and at least one entire Myrtle Beech tree have been brought down. I was intrigued by the sheer profusion of mosses, lichens and other plant growth on these ancient branches and I photographed the rich range of colour and texture in all shades of green since nowhere was the nature of the supporting branch revealed, so dense was the cover of these epiphytes.

Along this relatively flat section of the Aire River, numerous ponds have been formed by rock barriers and in one case by a mass of logs. The trunks of tree ferns, eucalypts and Myrtle Beeches have been piled up to make a most effective dam wall. Behind these barriers there were some beautiful reflections in the still water of tree ferns, water ferns and the gnarled trunks of the Myrtle Beeches.

At the base of one of these beeches I found a curiously tiered fungus about six centimetres high – *Podoserpula pusio* – a succession of light yellow

long caps borne on a slightly pink coloured stem. The undersurface was an ivory colour and, rather than gills, it had folds which has led to doubt as to whether it is a toadstool or in fact a member of the Bracket Fungi.

On my way back to the car park in the reserve I passed several huge gnarled Myrtle Beeches and wondered at their age. Many of the original Myrtle Beech trees have survived because the wood had limited commercial value and the dense wet gullies where they occur were seldom razed by fire. Since the oldest surviving Mountain Ash trees are said to be 300 years old, it is quite conceivable that these Myrtle Beeches, though much smaller, could be of the same vintage.

The trees accompanying the Myrtle Beech were mostly Satinwoods, although it was difficult to be sure exactly what they were, particularly when the leaves are confined to the topmost branches. All the tree ferns here appear to be Soft Tree Ferns whereas the ground layer is densely covered by Hard Water Fern very dark green in colour with large tough fronds. The steeper banks are clothed in Ruddy Ground Fern with a very profuse covering of bronze hairs on its foliage. One Soft Tree Fern was host to two tiny ferns established at the base: a Finger Fern and Mother Spleenwort.

Before returning home I visited the Hopetoun Falls. The weather by now was beginning to deteriorate and light rain was falling. With the recent heavy rains the falls were an impressive sight. It was slippery and awkward carrying my heavy gear down the steep track. However, it was worthwhile and, whilst I got very wet and fell into the river on one occasion, I managed what should prove to be some interesting photographs of these large falls. The five separate jets of water which characterise the falls during dry periods had this afternoon merged into one single roaring cascade. The spray generated by the falling water was such that everything within 50 metres of its base was covered in fine spray.

On my way home I passed a flock of 20 or so Yellow-tailed Black Cockatoos on some pine trees. They were settled in the tops of the pines and seemed to be searching for food, presumably pine nuts. This is the largest group of Black Cockatoos I have seen so far in the Otways.

AUGUST

*LEFT: A violent winter storm makes
its way towards the Sherbrook River.*

*ABOVE: Rock colours in the cliffs at
Moonlight Beach.*

3 AUGUST

On my way to Moonlight Bay early this morning I was impressed by the mass of dead bracken fronds along the roadside. The older fronds tend to die off in winter but there will be many new shoots to take their place in the following spring. Bracken is a plant which responds to disturbance, and roadsides provide the sort of unstable environment it likes, with occasional earthmoving operations, clearing and regular burning all contributing. In situations where firing is very frequent, bracken may dominate the understorey to the exclusion of almost all else.

I had always been led to believe that bracken, which occurs worldwide,

The cliffs at Moonlight Beach.

140

was a single species of plant. However, despite their close similarity, several separate species of bracken are now recognised as occurring throughout the world. Bracken spreads mainly by the means of underground stems or rhizomes and rarely by the spores located on the undersides of the fronds. The resilience of bracken is dependent on the rhizome's ability to survive burning, regular cutting and grazing.

The huge cliffs above Moonlight Beach are dramatic and grim, particularly at high tide with huge seas pounding against them. In places they are a mass of bulges and depressions where cannonball concretions have left clean hemispherical cups after being scooped out of the rock wall. The colour tends to vary across the concretions from an orange shade at the periphery to a green colour at the centre where they have been split open. At one point a few hundred metres west of the Racecourse Steps, I came across thin layers of what appeared to be charcoal but would almost certainly be coal. It lies embedded in the rock just above the level of the beach and perhaps 90 metres below the top of the cliffs. These very small deposits of coal would be considerably older than the brown-coal beds in the Tertiary sediments that are now being mined at Anglesea.

I noted the large bubbles which often form around objects on beaches as the waves retreat. They are very like soap bubbles and display the opalescent hues associated with oil slicks. I am uncertain as to what causes these bubbles, whether they are due to dissolved organic matter from decaying seaweed or the remains of crustacea or fish or even a spillage of oil in Bass Strait.

Later in the day, on my way back from the Devils Kitchen, I stopped to photograph an anchor and some other iron remnants from the wreck

Anchor from the wreck of the Marie Gabrielle *in 1868.*

141

of the *Marie Gabrielle*. This ship, a three-masted barque bound from Foochow to Melbourne with a cargo of tea, was driven ashore off what is now known as Wreck Beach at 1 am on 25 November 1869. The *Marie Gabrielle* luckily passed between two groups of rocks and ran aground on the sand, and her crew all reached shore safely.

Captain Blanchard, the mate and three crewmen set out for Cape Otway Lighthouse, 30 kilometres to the east. Bearing in mind this extraordinarily rugged coastline and the dense bushland flanking it, this must have been a hellish trip. Even today, with numerous access tracks and patches of clear pastureland, the coastline here still offers a challenge to the most determined bushwalkers. To negotiate the steepest cliffs, the party tore their clothing in pieces and made ropes to lower themselves to the shoreline below. The group arrived at the lighthouse in great distress having been without food for four days. Despite their hardships, however, this was one of the few shipwrecks in which no lives were lost.

7 AUGUST

This morning I noted a flock of about 50 egrets. They were smaller than the Great Egret and, although difficult to identify positively from a distance, they would almost certainly have been Cattle Egrets. These birds live on insects disturbed in the pastures by grazing animals. The Cattle Egret is an immigrant to Australia from the northern hemisphere. Its mode of living is closely adapted to that of introduced grazing animals, particularly cattle. The Cattle Egret relies on them not only to expose pasture insects but also as another source of food in the form of the various parasites which infest livestock.

The Common Heath was out in great abundance along Forest Road at Anglesea. This road runs north from the main Geelong–Anglesea Road and for the first few kilometres follows the line dividing cleared pastureland and the original heathy woodland. It was noticeable how the clearing of a firebreak some 25 metres in width between road and woodland has created apparently ideal conditions for the proliferation of Common Heath. The open strip is at this moment a pink and white carpet of flowers, whereas the neighbouring understorey of woodland which is less exposed to sunlight, reveals much smaller, scattered displays of heath.

It is noticeable how Golden Wattle has sprung up, presumably since the Ash Wednesday fire. It is not clear whether this species is endemic to the Anglesea heath and it has been suggested that it was introduced, probably for tanning purposes many years ago. Another plant, which is an introduction, is a species of Maritime Pine (*Pinus pinasta*). Lighter in foliage and colour than the more commonly grown Radiata Pine (*Pinus radiata*) and with a more open appearance, it is widely scattered through the Anglesea heathland. It was planted along with Radiata Pine as part of a pine planting program initiated before the Second World War. Probably some of these trees are remnants of those old plantations, most of which have disappeared as a result of fire. In most cases the plantations have now reverted to native vegetation. However, some of these pines, in view of their scattered positions, must have generated from seed. This species of pine is a native of the western Mediterranean where it grows in deep infertile sands. It can thus adapt easily to the nutrient-deficient soils of the Anglesea heathland, certainly

Leafless Bitter-pea (Daviesia brevifolia*).

LEFT: *Winter morning, Anglesea.*

ABOVE: *Needle Hakea* (Hakea sericea).

more so than Radiata Pine from Northern California which does not spread in this environment.

One plant I found in flower intrigued me. It was the Leafless Bitter-pea. This plant has no leaves, the orange-red pea flowers being attached to a narrow green cylindrical stem armed with sharp points. Nearby was another spiny plant, Needle Hakea, not yet in flower although the buds were well formed. In this latter case, the plant has leaves but these are reduced to very long, hard needlelike appendages which are extremely sharp. They will inflict a painful prick should you contact one unexpectedly while pushing through the undergrowth.

Thinking about this today and looking at other plants also with small hard prickly leaves, such as Prickly Tea Tree and Prickly Moses wattle, emphasised to me how common this feature is in the heath community. Prickly plants such as the ones described are said to be scleromorphic and

ABOVE: *The spring flowering leafless Globe Pea* (Sphaerolobium vimineum).

BELOW: *Bracket Fungus* (Stereum ostrea).

are a widespread and characteristic feature of the Australian flora; one that has reached its highest development in soils of very low fertility, usually sands. This is believed to be due to the lack of essential elements, especially phosphorus, the Australian continent generally having very low level of soil phosphorus. It may also reflect low levels of soil nitrogen. Nitrogen is an element added in part to the soil by the activity of nitrogen-fixing bacteria which in turn require phosphorus.

Some families of plants growing in these impoverished soils have been evolving since early Tertiary times, perhaps 50 million years ago. They have proliferated into a great number of species, utilising fewer plant cells as a response to the scarcity of essential chemical elements. And so plant species with small rigid leaves, short distances between the leaves (the internodes), and small size predominate.

At the Cumberland River I retraced my steps of some weeks ago to Jebbs Pool, a kilometre or two above the caravan park. I spent some hours photographing the river in the stretches above the pool. Here there are some beautiful tall and stately Manna Gums, their white trunks turning yellow at the base, scattered amongst the tree ferns and tall dense stands of Hazel Pomaderris mixed with Austral Mulberry and Musk. There are no waterfalls on this gentler stretch of the river, but in places the river runs swiftly through a series of rapids and deeper pools.

I found a beautiful group of yellow-orange Bracket or Shelf Fungi on a log. I think it is one of the Stereum species and, although very common, I have not been able to match it with any photographs in textbooks. There was a very dense accumulation of ground ferns of several species among the understorey of Hazel Pomaderris. Two prominent kinds were a species of Fishbone Water Fern and Mothershield Fern. The former, with fronds up to a metre in length, dominates the undergrowth here along the banks of the Cumberland and virtually nothing grows beneath it. In other places, often further back from the stream, Mothershield Fern is very common.

LEFT: *Water cascades over rocks at Jebbs Pool.*

ABOVE: *Small toadstools* (Mycena *sp) accumulate large water droplets.*

An elegant dark-green fern with very small pinnae, it has a covering of light brown hairs and is relatively hard to the touch. Presumably the mother in the name is derived from the characteristic development of small new plants near the end of the fronds from the buds called bulbils. In one case I examined two light-green pinnae about five centimetres long which had emerged from a bulbil, from whence a series of dark roots hung down below the mature frond.

On the way back to the car on a rocky exposure along the track, Small Rasp Fern was very much in evidence. What attracted my attention was not the characteristic harsh and green nature of the mature fronds but the very soft salmon pink colour of the young fronds, an unexpected splash of new colour in what was essentially an overwhelmingly green environment.

12 AUGUST

I was on my way at five-thirty this morning. It was pitch dark but the sky was clear and there was an excellent showing of stars.

A few kilometres before Winchelsea I pulled up quickly to take the opportunity to enjoy some reflections in a large dam on the northwest side of the road. The view was out over the vast Western District volcanic plain with the silhouette of Mount Elephant just visible in the far distance. There were some very interesting light effects on the still water caught by the rising sun. A lone Black Swan cruised slowly in the water on the far side of the dam and a pair of Chestnut Teal took off noisily and wheeled around before landing again in a paddock nearby and surveying me suspiciously.

This vast flat landmass of the Western District caused me to ponder why these basalt plains carry so few native trees. Stretching almost unbroken for 190 kilometres west of Melbourne, they have always been open grassy plains. Even in 1839 in the better watered parts around Camperdown, George Russell noted 'the great extent of deep rich soil measuring hundreds of acres being almost without trees on them'. And it was for this very reason that these plains were the first areas in Victoria to be exploited for grazing in the 1830s and 1840s.

The treeless state is generally attributed to the high clay content of the soil, a feature the Western District plains share with other great treeless plains of the world, like the prairies of North America. They are more impervious than other soils to the downward movement of water and to the deeper roots of trees; it is only in favoured spots along streams or on the slopes of old volcanoes that trees naturally ever took hold. Presumably

A chilly winter sky near Anglesea.

FAR LEFT: *Pouched Coral Fern*
(Gleichenia dicarpa), *Carlisle*
Heath.

LEFT: *Deformed spike of Austral*
Grass Tree (Xanthorrhoea
australis).

FOLLOWING PAGE: *Reflections*
in a farm dam near Winchelsea.

the soil profile of the few basalt hills is less consolidated and more porous than the plains, and tree roots can penetrate and expand to tap a larger volume of soil and moisture. The settlers eventually discovered suitable trees from other areas, such as the Sugar Gum and the Monterey Cypress, and cultural techniques that have enabled the plantation cover of trees to be established on the volcanic plains in the last 100 years.

That afternoon in the Carlisle State Park, 15 kilometres southwest of Gellibrand, I walked into the heath and was surprised at its height and density. With a higher rainfall than the comparable heathy woodland at Anglesea – 1,000 millimetres compared to 600 millimetres – the upper layers of plants were a metre or more above the ground and were hard to push through.

Nearby in a gully there was a very dense cover of Pouched Coral Fern. It had managed to climb over all the underlying plants and to dominate the creek-bed vegetation, forming a delicate green veil over everything else.

The road through the park passes over a high ridge which provides limited views to the east and to the southeast. It reveals the vegetation to be broadly broken up into wooded sections with heath as an understorey, and patches of open heath, some of which appear to be in drainage systems, with the outline of numerous small creeks etched in darker green. The darker colour comes from the Scented Paperbark and Coral Fern. Numerous gravel pits to the east along the ridge reveal the white, sandy and sterile nature of the soil here, and explain why this country was not opened up for settlement. It forms part of old Tertiary sand beds lying along the southwest edge of the older and more fertile Cretaceous sediments, which make up the main dome of the Otway Ranges.

Because of its strategic situation – it lies in the path of the prevailing winds that blow over the Otway Ranges – the Carlisle heathland has been heavily and repeatedly burnt to protect the valuable farmland and forests to the east from bushfires. Fires in the past have usually been driven in from the low-lying country to the west. Regular firing has almost certainly reduced the abundance of certain plants and invertebrate fauna and the rare Ground Parrot is no longer thought to be present here. It does not appear, however, to have adversely influenced many of the heath and tree species which flourish following fire. The regeneration of heath is remarkable.

The dominant eucalypt species, Shining Peppermint, Brown Stringybark and Messmate are fire tolerant, with heat-resistant bark and lignotubers, and they show no sign of having been reduced by the unnatural frequency of fires.

In these heathy woodlands, fire acts as a stimulant to new growth. It encourages the shooting of epicormic buds beneath the bark, and ensures the release of seeds from the woody fruits of other species. Heating of the soil by fire stimulates seed stored in the ground. In experiments on heathland, it has been shown that physical clearing of the vegetation leads to less than one per cent of the seedlings germinating when compared to burning.

I detoured along a dirt track leading west beyond Carlisle River to examine more closely an area of heathland. It traverses a peat soil and the heath itself was tall and dense. Along the track at the base of the heath species were a group of fernlike plants, Swamp Selaginella. Selaginellas are members of Lycopsida, plants that are related to ferns. Seldom more than a few centimetres tall today, Lycopsida of the early Tertiary period included large trees. The leaves are often small and like mosses possess just a single vein. The spore-bearing organs, the sporangia, are located at the base of leaves called sporophylls. Selaginellas have two types of spores and club mosses one. The Swamp Selaginella is a very dainty plant a few centimetres in height and with pinnate foliage. Today these displayed not only shades of green but a rich range of autumn colours through light brown to apricot to pink.

On a road-cutting nearby I found some specimens of the Slender Clubmoss which is related to the selaginellas but distinguished by its more upright growth and forked stems. It is apparently often found on such bare disturbed ground where it acts as a coloniser before other plants move in and take over.

Beyond the hamlet of Chapple Vale, a road runs southeast to Lavers Hill. The bushland just beyond the turnoff has recently been burnt and there is now a mass flowering of Austral Grass Trees. Today most plants sported huge single flowering heads, most just coming into flower. On the whole these were dead straight and up to three metres in height, but a few were twisted into strange shapes. In younger Austral Grass Tree plants or in those which naturally do not have trunks, it is suspected that ethylene produced during bushfires acts as a flowering stimulant to activate the growing apex located some 20 or 30 centimetres below the ground. Is it possible that the ethylene, a plant hormone, also accounts for the strange twisted shapes? Hormone weedicides also produce deformities which are the plants' response to an overdose of hormone.

Bushfires in grass-tree dominated heathland are greatly stimulated by the resins in this plant and the resulting devastation could be judged by the pure white, bare sand left between the individual grass trees. The first herb plants taking up the task of colonisation were prostrate Scented Sundews, many with a single white flower. Yet I would imagine by November there will be many more species of flowering plants to add colour to the scene.

On the roadside below the burnt grass trees I photographed a large plant of Needle Hakea in full flower. It is an extraordinarily prickly plant and I managed after much painful effort to remove one of the large woody fruits which, on being left on the car dashboard in the sun for an hour, sprang open to reveal a beautifully marked seed chamber in shades of red-brown and cream. I imagine this drying effect would be similar to that produced by quick fire. The seed falls from the open fruit after fire has raced through to produce seedlings in the succeeding spring months.

19 AUGUST

Wattles of various species, mostly those planted along the roadsides, are now everywhere in evidence in various shades of yellow and gold. But the Golden Wattle (*Acacia pycnantha*) has the most spectacular blossoms: masses of bright golden spheres one centimetre in diameter, closely bunched at the ends of the leafy branches. Also, unlike many wattles, it has an attractive perfume.

The show of flowers along the forest road near Anglesea is now at its best, and is dominated by Common Heath and Myrtle Wattle, with several other species just coming into flower. These included a Twining Fringe lily, Gorse Hakea, Grey Parrot-pea and Pink Bells. On the track which runs west from Forest Road and descends into the valley of the Anglesea

Golden Wattle (Acacia pycnantha*)*.

151

ABOVE LEFT: *Male flowers of Scrub She-oak* (Allocasuarina paludosa).

ABOVE RIGHT: *Female flowers and cones of Scrub She-oak* (Allocasuarina paludosa).

River, a number of small stunted eucalypts were also beginning to flower.

As I ate my lunchtime sandwiches, I contemplated, like a landscape artist, the shape and the colour of the heathland, and found it strangely lacking in strong greens. The dominant shades today were the browns and the fawns of the rushes, sedges and grasses, and the muted greens contributed by the foliage of bush peas, heath, tea trees and Scrub She-oaks. These latter colours were dull olive or grey-green. The strong colour highlights came from vivid yellow clumps of Myrtle Wattle and the erect cylindrical heads of the pink, white, and red flowers of Common Heath. The real interest and the peculiarly Australian content of the scene was provided by the burnt and twisted trunks of eucalypts with their strange and arresting colours. The coal-black bark had been replaced by fresh grey bark, and there were orange patches where it had been removed by trees rubbing against each other in the wind or where it had been torn away, perhaps by possums.

I photographed the male flower of the Scrub She-oak – small cylindrical rust-brown bunches on green stems. There were no female flowers in these examples but she-oaks can bear both male and female flowers on the one plant (monoecious) or on separate plants (dioecious). She-oaks belong to the family Casuarinaceae which has similarities with pines and cypresses. Like pines and cypresses, pollination in she-oaks depends on wind-borne pollen landing on female flowers.

In photographing the opening flower buds of the Gorse Hakea I was started to find a colourful larva of a cup moth, one of the so-called Chinese Junk caterpillars. I was surprised that it would be feeding on hakea and I believe that it probably crawled off a leaf of the unidentified eucalypt growing next to the hakea. I have never seen these caterpillars feeding on anything other than eucalypts before, although some species of cup moth (family Limacodidae) do feed on members of the Proteacea family, such as banksias and grevilleas.

During its life history, the cup moth protects itself with two quite different mechanisms: in the larval or caterpillar stage by means of the effective, and very painful sting, the paired organs containing bundles of yellow spines; and in the pupal stage, the more or less spherical and very tough cocoon. These cocoons are spun from silk by the caterpillar then hardened with a varnishlike secretion.

Nearby I eventually located the cause of the near defoliation of some eucalypt saplings. It was a cluster of 20 or 30 large (30 millimetres) sawfly larvae which were quickly aware of my presence and soon rearing backwards, each exuding a strong eucalypt-smelling fluid. This unpleasant habit has given rise to their popular name of spitfires. The larvae looked very close to maturity and will shortly leave the tree and pupate in mass in a depression in the ground. The name for this primitive family of wasps is derived from the sawlike appendage with which the female cuts a slit in the leaf to lay her eggs.

Sawfly larvae are able to extract eucalyptus oil from the leaves and to store it in their foregut. When disturbed, they regurgitate the liquid, often with a flicking movement which, en masse, not only produces a powerful odour but also the appearance of a frightening mass of moving limbs. Tests have shown that the fluid is highly unpalatable to predators of various kinds, including meat ants and birds, and it is undoubtedly an effective defensive weapon. Surprisingly large quantities of fluid are retained in the pouch of the foregut and may make up to 20 per cent of the weight of mature larvae. On pupation the fluid is utilised for silk in the construction of the cocoon and so continues to protect the insect in this immobile and vulnerable phase of its existence.

The utilisation of eucalyptus oil by sawflies is in some ways an ironic twist. It is generally believed that eucalypts, along with many other types

ABOVE: *Close up of the paired stinging organs of a cup moth larva* (Doratifera *sp*).

BELOW: *Larva of a cup moth* (Doratifera *sp*).

ABOVE LEFT: Dwarf Greenhoods (Pterostylis nana).

ABOVE RIGHT: Tall Greenhoods (Pterostylis longifolia) *flowers, topmost open and lower one closed.*

BELOW: Sawfly lavae (Perga *sp*).

of plants with distasteful chemicals in their foliage, developed these during their evolution as a means of protection against insects. Some leaf-eating insects, however, have evolved so they can tolerate eucalyptus oil and, in the case of sawflies, have learnt to use it for their own protection.

At an orchid patch near Gumflat I soon located several groups of Dwarf Greenhoods. As the name suggests, they are tiny in stature, rarely reaching 10 centimetres in height. They have a quaint-looking flower and the hood, or galea, is a translucent milky white with bold green stripes down its length, and the vertically-held lower sepal is surmounted by two erect filaments over a centimetre in length. They look for all the world like antennae and give the orchid, which grows from a rosette of tiny leaves, an insectlike appearance. I noted that they were growing in relatively open, partially sunlit situations, unlike other greenhood species which are usually found in shade.

Later I located a smaller and isolated patch of the Tall Greenhood. As the name suggests, this species can grow quite tall for a native orchid – sometimes up to 90 centimetres – although those I have found today were only about 30 centimetres. The tongue or labellum of this orchid, which varies greatly in the number of flowers carried on the one plant, is very sensitive and with a touch of a twig can be made to spring shut suddenly. This is what happens when the pollinating vector, a midge or fungal gnat, enters the flower seeking nectar at the base of the labellum. It is forced to walk over the female part, the stigma, and picks up the pollen. As it escapes out of the top of the hood, it brushes past the conveniently placed pollen-bearing anthers or pollinia and so conveys pollen to the next flower it visits.

22 & 23 AUGUST

My family joined me today and we left home at 6.40 pm to stay overnight at Kangaroobie, a holiday farm at Princetown.

Below Kangaroobie lies a large swamp forming part of the flood plain immediately before the outlet of the Gellibrand River at Point Ronald. Except for some small patches of open water near the Great Ocean Road, the swamp is choked with reeds.

The next morning I went out early to see what bird life I could find on the swamp. A solitary Great Egret occupied the small lake and floated majestically and somewhat aloofly on the water at the western end, providing an interesting foreground to a wintry sunrise scene. Nearby, but staying very close to the dense wall of reeds, two Black Swans and six furry grey cygnets swam tentatively along.

A pair of Chestnut Teal viewed me suspiciously as I peered into the reeds trying to locate their chicks which could be heard chirping busily. The chicks were very well camouflaged and protected by the tall dense rushes. Coastal wetlands are a favourite location of Chestnut Teal which are often seen in flocks with Grey Teal.

Later in the morning, at a point further up the Gellibrand River, we found a huge old bush of African Boxthorn which proved to be a veritable dormitory for a flock of Red-browed Finches all chattering furiously as they flew away. These birds seem extraordinarily gregarious and apparently like to nest in numbers in bushes such as this one.

Nearby we walked across an old bridge over the Gellibrand River, which at this stage of its course is very slow-flowing as it meanders over its extensive flood plain. Though none were to be seen today, the river apparently harbours a rich variety of native fish, including small galaxias, Black Fish, Tupong, Australian Bass and Bullhead Minnow, as well as Short-finned Eels.

The purpose of our trek was to visit the site of Rivernook, a famous guesthouse founded last century which was demolished in the 1950s. Now only a few old gnarled cypresses and clumps of daffodils, jonquils and Michaelmas Daisies are all that remain among the rich green grass of the surrounding paddock. Yet here was once a homestead that played host to

many notable people. The popular and gregarious proprietor of Rivernook, Evans, also provided shelter and food for the survivors of the barque *Fiji*, wrecked at nearby Moonlight Beach. Apparently many relics of shipwrecks from along the coast were kept on display at the guesthouse.

The mouth of the Gellibrand, like other rivers running down from the Otways, is often blocked by a sand bar, particularly during late summer and autumn. After heavy spring rain the water builds up in the swamp near the entrance and eventually, with the aid of storm waves, it breaks out and cuts through. The waves pound in here with great force and it is hard to believe that there was any local boat traffic between the inlet and the ocean. There are signs of an old breakwater with an odd stump still sticking out of the sand. Apparently efforts were made to assist the flow of the river to the sea by means of a tunnel through the high west-facing cliff of Point Ronald and by construction of a breakwater, but both schemes failed to tame the powerful forces of nature.

Charles La Trobe noted the vagaries of this river when, as Superintendent of the Port Phillip District, he made his epic journeys to open a route to Cape Otway. His aim was to establish a lighthouse on this key coastal prominence and so reduce the tragic toll of shipwrecks. On the second of his trips in December 1845, La Trobe wrote that the party 'waited for the fall of the tide' before proceeding. However, on his third and successful venture four months later, he recorded that when they reached the Gellibrand, they came 'to a dead halt, the whole valley being to our surprise, one wide lake'. Unable to get the horses over the river, La Trobe left one member, Trooper Bird, behind to keep watch over their horses and provisions. By partially stripping, with their kit and provisions on their heads, they

Early winter morning at the swamp near the mouth of the Gellibrand River.

157

RIGHT: *Old limpet shell*
(Cellana *cf* solida).

BELOW: *Moth larvae*
(unidentified).

eventually made the crossing to the eastern bank of the river. Two days later they became the first Europeans to reach Cape Otway.

That evening we visited Melba Gully just southwest of Lavers Hill to see the glow-worms. It was not a happy beginning to our outing when we discovered we could not light a fire no matter how hard we tried. Other visitors had the same problem. The wood provided by the park ranger was either too green or too damp and no amount of fanning would make it burn; so in the end we had to content ourselves with a cold, dark and windy dinner party. The glow-worms, however, lived up to their reputation and were a great sight, looking like so many stars in a clear sky. They were easier to see on the banks above the walking track but could be found almost anywhere there was some exposed face, whether it was soil or rock. Close examination did not reveal any of the creatures causing the light but it would have required better illumination than we had. The insects responsible are the larvae of fungus gnats (*Arachnocampa* sp). They live in wet situations, usually in cracks in rock faces, and attract their tiny insect prey by the phosphorescent light they produce and trap them in a hanging veil of threads dotted with small beads of moisture.

The luminosity of the larvae of fungus gnats must be distinguished from that of the better known fireflies which are in fact beetles (Lampyridae). Fireflies, mostly found in tropical regions, are able to control the light they emit in a series of flashes. In some remarkable way in certain species the flashes can actually be synchronised among a group of beetles, one apparently answering another. The reasons for the luminosity may be different but in both cases it is pretty basic – fireflies use their night lights as a means of sexual attraction, fungus gnats as a means of catching prey.

*The dew-dropped web of the glow-worm (*Arachnocampa *sp).*

159

SEPTEMBER

LEFT: Late afternoon on the lower reaches of the Aire River.

ABOVE: Tiger Orchid (Diuris sulphurea) and hoverfly (Syrphidae).

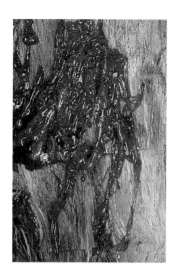

ABOVE: Resin on trunk of Messmate (Eucalyptus obliqua).

BELOW: Spring pastures near Lavers Hill.

1 SEPTEMBER

My destination this morning was Cape Otway and on the way I stopped to capture on film a striking view of farmland 10 kilometres east of Lavers Hill. The country near the road has been cleared and low rays of the sun highlighted the rounded contours of the pastures which are now carrying crossbred ewes and lambs. They were dotted all over the pasture but were not frightened by my presence, even when I was only a few metres from the fence.

I photographed some bright red solidified exudate of resin which had oozed from the trunk of a Messmate. I am not sure why some trees produce resin but you see it frequently on various species of eucalypt. It may be as a result of injury but if it is, the injury is not obvious. The resin hung down like a red lustrous veil of stalactites and glistened brilliantly wherever sunlight caught it.

Above the Parker River estuary, the previously cleared farmland has been reinvaded by Coast Beard Heath. Individual bushes are widely separated and it is easy to walk between them on the old pasture. Today the Coast Beard Heath was in full bloom: masses of small, white, strongly scented flowers capping the yellow-green foliage a metre or two in height. It was a perfect start to spring, a clear sunny day, the fragrance of the beard heath hanging heavily in the air and a mass of Painted Lady and Australian Admiral butterflies and yellow-banded hoverflies feeding at the blossoms.

On the shore platform bordering the entrance to the Parker River, large expanses of bright green seaweed have taken hold since my last visit some months ago. It must be seasonal in its growth because I walked over and photographed these same rocks on my last visit and saw no sign of this seaweed. It looks superficially much like the very common green seaweed (*Enteromorpha intestinalis*) which is harvested as a bait for fishing. I had not imagined seaweed as responding to the seasons. However, even though the range of ocean temperatures is smaller than that on land, it is still significant. There is no reason why the growth of seaweeds, which are marine algae, would not be influenced both by changes in temperature and light.

I found a lone specimen of a species of daisy, the Variable Groundsel, growing on the cliff face. Its bright yellow flowers had attracted a number of hoverflies. Hoverflies are often beelike in appearance and one species is known actually to fly with the bees that it mimics, presumably to gain a protective advantage against its predators. The species I photographed, however, was not particularly like a bee but rather like a small wasp. I doubt that it can be a mimic because it is so very common. Mimicry can only be sustained if the mimic is considerably rarer than the model – no more than 10 per cent of its number – otherwise the predator soon discovers the ruse.

From the Parker River estuary I took the dirt road back towards Cape Otway and turned off down a very narrow bush track to Point Franklin about four kilometres east of the lighthouse. The country immediately to the north of the point is made up of sand dunes which merge into the

163

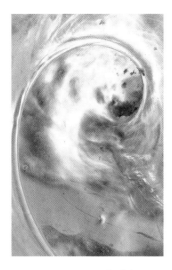

ABOVE: Detail of the inner surface of an abalone or ear shell (Haliotis sp).

RIGHT: Turban Shell (Turbo undulatus).

BELOW: Clouds float across a morning sky at Point Franklin.

low heathy undergrowth some hundreds of metres further inland. These dunes overlie the Cretaceous sediments exposed as low cliffs in places on the east side of Point Franklin. A very wide apron is provided by a shore platform on the southwest side. On this shelf, masses of kelp had accumulated and glistened like polished ebony in the sun.

The view west from Point Franklin towards the lighthouse across Oyster Bay encapsulates the feeling of the Otway coast more effectively than any other I know: the partly concealed and dangerous Otway Reef visible just out to sea from the Cape, huge waves crashing on partly submerged rocks, spray rising many metres into the air, and the whole scene dominated by the lighthouse perched on a cliff 80 metres above the sea. It evokes at

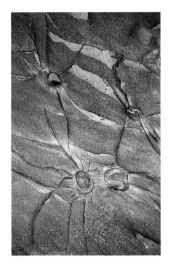

LEFT: *Exposed limestone sand dunes, Point Franklin.*

ABOVE: *Patterns in the sandstone, Point Franklin.*

once the power of one of the world's most turbulent seas and a sense of danger and foreboding. Close to where I photographed this scene lies part of the wreck of *Eric the Red*, a ship that went down on the Otway Reef on 4 September 1880 whilst bringing 500 tonnes of exhibits from the United States for the first International Exhibition held in Melbourne that year. A large portion of the wreck was driven onto the eastern side of Point Franklin and even though not visible today, the anchor can apparently still be seen at low tide wedged between the rocks.

All but one crew member and a passenger managed to escape from the wreck, some in a boat and most of the remainder clinging to what was left of the poop deck and the mizzenmast. By extraordinary good fortune the steamer *Dawn*, which travelled regularly between Melbourne and Warrnambool, made the journey one day earlier than scheduled. Again by the utmost good luck, the lookout on the *Dawn* thought he heard voices as they passed Cape Otway in the dark at four in the morning. The captain responded by halting the ship and eventually the boatload of four survivors was then taken on board. Later a further 17, including the captain, were picked up still clinging to the mizzenmast. Four, including one passenger, were lost and the only body recovered is buried in the cemetery at Cape Otway.

Hugh Gibson, who lived 40 kilometres to the west at Glenample, recorded in his memoirs how the beaches were strewn for a distance of 30 miles with an incredible array of cargo, including drums of oil and kerosene and boxes of tobacco, rifles, revolvers and watches. Needless to say, this rich bounty attracted an army of fossickers, some from as far afield as Bendigo, Geelong and Melbourne.

The disaster was difficult to explain because the captain and first mate had seen the Otway light only minutes before the ship struck the reef and yet they estimated its distance to be six miles or more. A haze, also noted by the captain of the *Dawn*, over the coast that evening may perhaps have diminished the intensity of the light and made it seem more distant.

I photographed some interesting patterns in the sand: closely repeated corrugations, some on built-up sections of sand on exposed rock and in one case an almost perfectly drawn circle cut by the long trailing leaves of Marram Grass driven by the incessant wind.

Snails are very common here. Some of the pioneering plants in the dune had been attacked by large colonies. They collect in groups around the plants and eventually demolish them. Judging by the number of accumulated shells, this is no small problem. I wondered if snail control is part of the program of dune stabilisation.

The snails are a species introduced from Europe. The Dune Snail has adapted itself to similar environments in Australia. Unfortunately, it is partial to the native plant species as well as introduced ones. A study some years ago set out to determine the reason for the Dune Snail's appearance as isolated colonies rather than as a widespread population. It drew the conclusion that this particular snail has little or no ability to spread itself and is dependent on man to introduce it to a dune accidentally and subsequently to disperse it. It was significant that the snails I saw today were in the one location along the natural pathway visitors take to reach the rocks at Point Franklin.

Inland from the foredunes I spent some time exploring a strange moonscape, bare of all vegetation save for the tops of dunes where clumps of Coastal

The Dune Snail (Theba pisana).

166

Daisy Bush still maintain a precarious toehold. Small chunks of limestone littered the ground in one place, an outcrop of these strangely shaped and textured rocks forming a strong foreground for a photograph. It is easy to see how you could mistake these chunks of limestone for fossilised trees as some do have the appearance of old worn tree stumps. It is believed that those with the appearance of tree stumps and limbs may in fact have been formed from limestone accumulating around the dead roots of shrubs.

Where the light dune sand had been blown away and a heavier underlying sand exposed, often orange-red in colour, swarms of small dark brown wasps were flying and crawling around small holes in the ground. Every so often one would plunge into a hole, disappear, then reappear within half a minute and fly off. Others seemed to be examining the holes more cautiously, sticking their head in and emerging suddenly as though warned off by an inmate. These digger wasps belong to the genus *Pison* and are parasitic on spiders which they first paralyse then store in underground nests as food for their larvae. The adult wasps are nectar feeders and it would seem that only the flowering Coast Beard Heath could provide a sufficient source of food for such a large population of wasps.

On a smooth stretch of white sandy beach which separates the bare dunes from the broad rocky shore platform at Point Franklin I came across two foraging Red-capped Plovers. They are very busy, dainty birds, the male easily identifiable from the otherwise very similar female by its rust red cap. My efforts to photograph them were continually frustrated by their habit of moving in quick bursts, always keeping the same distance from the camera. They were later joined by four larger birds, all Hooded Plovers. They too proved to be a moving target for the camera but were happy to gather on the rock platform and to view me rather suspiciously from the edge of the rocks. The Hooded Plovers made an interesting picture with their red bills and beaks and white plumage, perched together against a background of breaking waves.

ABOVE: A digger wasp (Pison sp).

BELOW: View of the coast east of Cape Volney.

167

Close-up of Common Beard Heath
(Leucopogon virgatus).

13 SEPTEMBER

Today I visited the heathy woodlands and open heath immediately to the east of Anglesea known as Demons Bluff. The cliffs here are extremely steep, virtually sheer. If you were to fall there would be absolutely nothing to grab onto on your way down to the narrow beach below. They have that unique Anglesea look with the dark banding of the carbonaceous sediments below the topmost ochre-coloured layers, and are unlike any cliffs between here and Warrnambool, though slightly reminiscent of the limestone cliffs of Port Campbell. The upper beds of the sedimentary rock at Anglesea are classified geologically as greywacke. It is a form of sandstone rich in tiny fossils called cyclammina now represented as tests or shells of the previously living creatures, members of the Protozoa.

I noticed that the vegetation does not extend right to the edge of the cliffs and there is a bare apron a couple of metres wide. I imagine this would be due to two factors: firstly, the exposure of soil on the cliff face would reduce its water-holding capacity and, secondly, damage from salt air and spray here would be at its maximum.

Along the seaward edge of the cliff, birds patrolled. Welcome Swallows mainly, their flight patterns graceful and interesting to watch. Several seconds of downward gliding is followed by a few quick wing beats, causing them to soar up the cliff face and then equally suddenly to drop down again. Swallows expend so much energy in this way attempting to catch small insects not visible to our eyes which are presumably borne up by the wind currents from the beach below.

I also saw a kestrel of fawn body colour, darker facings and swept-back wings as it set out from its rocky perch several metres below the edge of the cliff. Later, several Pacific Gulls flew by along the beach some 100 metres below the clifftop. The only other birds I saw were a group of magpies foraging in the heath behind the cliff.

The bright yellow flowering daisy, African Boneseed, has found a niche on the clifftops at Demons Bluff, although it is thus far confined to the disturbed and eroded section above the cliffs where people walk. I could not see any other plants on the heathland, but it may be hard to contain if these established plants are not removed.

Boneseed is an unusual weed in that it does not pose an agricultural problem. It cannot compete with vigorous pastures or crops, but it is a menace in reservations of native bushland because of its ability to establish itself after any physical disturbance, and even over longer periods in undisturbed natural situations. The name is derived from the small, hard, spherical, bone-coloured seeds produced singly from each fruit. Boneseed is spread by birds that eat the fruit, by rabbits and perhaps even by ants. Regrettably, there is also evidence that its dissemination may be encouraged by the dumping of garden refuse.

A handsome plant, it was first brought to Australia in 1858 when it was planted in the Botanic Gardens in Melbourne. It has since spread widely but so far is only a threat in localities south of Melbourne. It is a native of the coastal dunes of South Africa where it is common enough. There it is presumably kept under control by a number of factors – probably a combination of insect, animal predation, and climate – and it causes no trouble.

There is evidence that Boneseed's proliferation accelerated during the 1950s and it has been suggested that this may have been due to the reduction of rabbit populations by myxomatosis. Although rabbits are recognised as being able to spread the seed, in large enough numbers they may have also suppressed the seedlings by eating them. Chemical control or elimination

of Boneseed is inappropriate in bushland where it would damage other valuable plant species. Pulling out plants, which is easy enough to do, tends to stimulate the germination of new seedlings from the bank of seeds still in the ground. Continually repeated, it would be possible, though very difficult, to eliminate Boneseed. Clearly the ideal would be a form of biological control and, unless some breakthrough in this direction occurs, it seems likely that some of our most valuable bushland may well go the way of the You Yangs, much of which has been spoiled by this weed. There is hope that a small black beetle, *Chrysolina progressai*, which in South Africa lives on Boneseed and another related weed, Bitou Bush, may be the answer. The beetle is being evaluated and could soon be released. With all its problems, Boneseed is a striking plant when in bloom. There was a large bush in flower on the edge of Demons Bluff today and it made an attractive foreground feature for a telephoto shot of the Anglesea township

Running Postman (Kennedia
prostrata).

over a kilometre away to the west.

Much of the flowering of the Common Heath has ceased. In its place a number of flowering species have come to life, including two small species of beard heath, Pink Bells, two species of yellow guinea flower, and the Rabbits Ears Orchid, which is not yet open. Some of the larger wattle species, including Golden Wattle and Coastal Wattle, are also in flower.

There was also a very bright display of the Running Postman in a disturbed and burnt area near the Ocean Road. Running Postman loves to spread out over bare ground after a fire. I found it climbing over a fired stump, the bright brick red and green centred flowers beautifully contrasted against the jet-black background of the stump. Following fire and with a minimum of competition, Running Postman always looks very luxuriant, whereas in unburnt bushland it has fewer, smaller flowers and small leaves of a duller green.

23 SEPTEMBER

It was very evident on the way down to Anglesea this morning that the wattles are now on the wane. Most species have either finished blooming or are fast fading.

I located a flowering Red Beaks Orchid which surprised me because they are so difficult to find in flower in the absence of fire. Last year, after much searching, I found a lone specimen but unfortunately it was

LEFT: *Pink Fairy Orchid*
(Caladenia latifolia) *with visiting
hoverfly* (Syrphidae).

ABOVE: *Red Beaks Orchid*
(Lyperanthus nigricans).

just past its flowering best. This plant I found today, however, was a superb example with at least six flowers on a single 20-centimetre stalk which had emerged from one single large round prostrate leaf. The effect of fire on this orchid is quite remarkable and WH Nicholls in his book *Orchids of Australia* notes that in one instance 100 flowering plants were counted on a single square metre of burnt ground!

The Red Beaks Orchid is one of a few Australian terrestrial orchids dependent on summer fires for mass flowering, although a few isolated individuals will flower in any year. The stimulus for flowering is likely to be hormonal and ethylene, which is produced in bushfires and triggers flowering in plants, is the most likely cause. The extra light available due to reduced competition from other plants and the release of nutrients by the so-called ash-bed effect can enhance the vigour of orchids after fire but cannot explain the initiation of flowering.

Before returning home I inspected a thicket of Moonah alongside the Anglesea River. The Pink Fairy Orchids were out in abundance in the dull light under the low canopy of the Moonahs. They were growing from a dense carpet of lichen and moss and other small plants including the round leaves of the Slaty Helmet Orchid. I noted yellow-and-black-bodied hoverflies visiting the Pink Fairy Orchids and was able to photograph one specimen as it examined the labellum of the orchid. I have seen hoverflies on closely allied species of spider orchids. It is a cosmopolitan insect and generally is not regarded as a significant pollinating vector of native orchids.

28 SEPTEMBER

This morning at Port Campbell was dull and windy with some light rain. I occupied my time again trying to locate the rare Swamp Diuris Orchid. Despite searching many low-lying areas I did not find a single specimen. I did, however, locate a Dwarf Boronia, a tiny prostrate plant with white flowers, growing on a cleared strip cut along the side of a dirt road which

runs from the Port Campbell rubbish tip easterly before turning north into the farmland. This particular section of heathland is dominated by Prickly Tea Tree and Scrub She-oak. It appears not to have been burnt for several years and in many places is over a metre high, the tea tree smothering any competition, from many species of herbaceous plants, including orchids. In future, fire management of these coastline heathlands will be critical to maintain a high level of floral diversity.

I hunted diligently for an hour or more on the heath on the western side of the Sherbrook River where the rare and very beautiful Metallic

Sun Orchid occurs. Whilst my search for this species also proved in vain I did find a bright yellow form of donkey orchid. I thought at first that this was the Swamp Diuris since it was growing in a damp patch of grassy country along a vehicle track. However, on checking my reference books on my return tonight, I now believe it is a Tiger Orchid, albeit a very yellow form with almost no dark markings visible.

At one stage, a New Holland Honeyeater alighted on the long flowering spike of a grass tree and, head downward, extracted nectar from the lower flowers before flying away. A little later near the steps down at the mouth of the Sherbrook River I saw in the distance what looked to be a pair of Yellow-faced Honeyeaters.

Huge seas were running at Broken Head and the spray was exploding upwards of 30 metres and drenching the top of the cliffs. Broken Head is ideally placed to catch the full force of the Bass Strait rollers with deep water running right up towards the cliff face, and today it demonstrated most graphically the great power of the ocean. I took time to photograph the towering plumes of spray from the vicinity of Loch Ard Gorge about a kilometre to the east.

A quick walk along the beach west of Sherbrook River later in the afternoon provided some opportunities for interesting photographs taken into the fast disappearing sun. Within a few minutes, huge storm clouds blew in and heavy rain began to fall. Before leaving the beach, I found and photographed a large dragonfly, drowned in the sea and washed up on shore. It was difficult to photograph as the wind constantly caught the wings and lifted them into the air.

*Seaweed (*Macrocystus angustifolia*).*

OCTOBER

LEFT: Early morning silhouette of Moonahs (Melaleuca lanceolata).

ABOVE: Australian Admiral butterfly (Vanessa itea).

11 OCTOBER

I noted a few birds on the way down to Urquhart Bluff early this morning and at Merrijig Creek I disturbed a small flock of Eastern Rosellas feeding along the roadway. They are always exciting to see with their beautiful apple-green colour mixed with flashes of red, blue and yellow, though this bird is neither as brilliant nor as common as the red and blue Crimson Rosella. Like a number of the parrots and cockatoos, Eastern Rosellas appear to have benefited from the clearing of forest and woodlands and the subsequent establishment of pastures and crops. These changes have presumably provided more seed for them to feed on and more of the open habitat which they prefer, in contrast to Crimson Rosellas which are found even in the densest forests of the Otways. I also noted a few lone magpies which often delay their takeoff from the road dangerously late and, as a result, are frequently seen dead along the roadside. It is interesting that neither crows nor Magpie Larks seem ever to get killed in this way.

As a result of the very low tide this morning and the large expanse of beach exposed at Urquhart Bluff, it was possible to see how much the sand has moved since my last visit here several months ago. Some of the very big boulders embedded in the beach are now almost entirely covered by sand. Here it is a temporary build-up, whereas a few kilometres east at Anglesea, the beach was eroded away dramatically a few years ago.

I found several groups of shells next to the rock pools. Pheasant shells were among the commonest and certainly the most striking. There are two species that occur here, one considerably larger than the other and which may reach six centimetres in length. They are probably the most attractive shells found on Victorian beaches.

Both species of pheasant shells are very variable in the colour of their whorled markings and no two specimens are exactly the same. They occur on exposed shore platforms, which provide the rock pools and the associated seaweeds on which they feed. Mixed in with the pheasant shells were tiny conical shells with bright opalescent inner surfaces revealed when the outer shell is chipped or worn. This has always been a very good shell locality and one of the few along this section of coastline.

Later I stopped at a burnt patch of heathy woodland on the seaward side of the Ocean Road not far from the Point Addis turnoff. The regrowth

BELOW: A very variably patterned pheasant shell (Phasianella ventricosa).

*RIGHT: Turban shell (*Turbo undulatus*) and pheasant shells* (Phasianella australis).

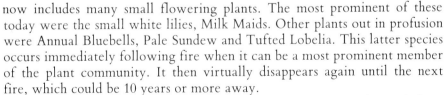

LEFT: *Wallflower* (Diuris Corymbosa) *Orchids flower in profusion following fire.*

ABOVE TOP: *Wallflower* (Diuris Corymbosa) *Orchid.*

ABOVE BOTTOM: *Milk Maids* (Burchardia umbellata) *flower after rain.*

now includes many small flowering plants. The most prominent of these today were the small white lilies, Milk Maids. Other plants out in profusion were Annual Bluebells, Pale Sundew and Tufted Lobelia. This latter species occurs immediately following fire when it can be a most prominent member of the plant community. It then virtually disappears again until the next fire, which could be 10 years or more away.

I noted a few large colonies of the Wallflower Diuris. The orchids in each case were closely massed and provided a good subject for photography against a background of burnt Messmate trunks. Other plants recovering from the autumn burn included a species of lomatia, Flat Pea, and the white Blunt Everlasting.

An Austral Grass Tree was in full flower with tall white creamy flowering stalks, two metres in length, but strangely it had attracted few insect visitors since the flowers had just opened. Normally you would expect to find a great variety of insects on a solitary flowering grass tree in this situation but today I could only find one introduced bee, an Australian Admiral butterfly and a small native fly which I was unable to identify.

14 OCTOBER

Today at Anglesea I located a species I was very keen to see again, the Bearded Greenhood. The flowers were on the wane but I was able to select one perfect specimen to photograph. The very prominent labellum of this orchid, covered with yellow hairs, protrudes far beyond the sepals which form the hood and makes it one of the most distinctive of our native terrestrial orchids.

There was a much greater variety of orchids, lilies and grasses in flower than three weeks ago. These plants, the monocotyledons, seem best able to fill the gap in the first year after fire, enjoying the lack of competition for sunlight and water from the larger heathland plants. In the second year a great many more heathland species appear and the third year after fire almost all will have returned. Some idea of the resilience of the Anglesea heathland to fire is the recovery measured after the devastating Ash Wednesday fire. Ground cover was a mere one per cent at the end of year one, but by year three it had reached 60 per cent.

A few large Common Spider Orchids were also in evidence but they were quite variable in shape, colour and size. Occasionally the variation comes about by hybridisation with the Green Comb Spider Orchid which flowers at the same time of the year and in the same locations.

Other flower species in this very colourful display were Blue Stars or Squill with prominent anthers, and many-flowered matrush with a grasslike flowering spike perhaps 12 centimetres long and with a subtle array of

colour from beige through orange to purple. The matrushes have, until recently, been classed as members of the lily family and are a common enough component of our heathland and heathy woodland flora. However, because the flowers are mostly unspectacular and bear no obvious resemblance to lilies, most people would see them as rushes or sedges. They are the food plant of a group of skipper butterflies which are also significant pollinators of several heath plants in these communities. In spring, you see them darting from one flower to the next with their long proboscises quickly uncurling to drink the nectar available in the flowers. Butterflies and bees, though in many instances visiting the same flowers, have different requirements. Bees utilise nectar as their primary source of carbohydrate and pollen to obtain protein, the bulk of the latter being used to feed their larvae, whereas butterflies can only make use of nectar. Where butterflies specialise in pollinating certain flowers it has been shown that these have a high amino acid content, so they gain some protein as well as carbohydrate from their all-liquid diet.

In a damp area recently burnt there were large groups of small flowering plants, mainly orchids, lilies and grasses. There were four species of sun orchids: Rabbits Ears, a Salmon Sun Orchid, the Twisted Sun Orchid and

TOP RIGHT: *Dotted Sun Orchid*
(Thelymitra ixioides).

RIGHT: *Salmon Sun Orchid*
(Thelymitra rubra).

the Dotted Sun Orchid. Fortunately, they were sufficiently open in the warm morning sunshine to enable me to photograph them. Other orchids we found included large white Common Spider Orchids among crowded patches of Hare Orchids, Yellow Onion Orchids and a single specimen of the Flying Duck Orchid. The Yellow Onion Orchids were growing in dense masses each no more than six centimetres high with their many minute flowers held tightly along the flowering spike.

In one depression I found a small patch of the Pygmy Club Moss, a species of club moss that responds to fire, often coming up in masses in heathland following a bushfire. The specimen I photographed today was less than five centimetres tall with narrow leaves around the bases of the fleshy stalk which bear the terminal fruiting body called a strobilus which contains several spore-bearing sporangia.

The three sundews, Scented Sundew, Tall Sundew and Pale Sundew, were common, though I noted only Tall Sundew in flower. Pale Sundew can be distinguished in flower from the very similar and upright growing Tall Sundew by its white rather than pink flowers and, when in bud, by the fact that the sepals of the Pale Sundew are hairy in comparison to those of the Tall Sundew. All three sundews grow together and I wondered whether they snare different species of insects since the two tall species and the prostrate Scented Sundew occupy different layers of air above the ground, or whether they are in competition with each other for the same species.

Where the fire had not burnt the Common Heath along the track it was noticeable that the plants were heavily in seed. Heath is one of those species that regrows by seed and for this reason does not strongly reassert itself in the heathland for about five years after fire. Most heathland species (70 per cent) regenerate vegetatively and thus can move in more quickly than Common Heath to fill the open spaces left by fire.

ABOVE LEFT: Hare Orchids (Leptoceras menziesii) *in profusion.*

ABOVE: Close-up of a Hare Orchid (Leptoceras menziesii).

17 OCTOBER

I left home at 6.35 am and arrived at a burnt patch of heathy woodland one kilometre southwest of the Point Addis turnoff. The early part of the day provided good weather with regular bursts of sunshine.

I spent some time watching a skipper butterfly, the Phigalia Skipper, as it briefly visited a Wallflower Orchid before quickly moving on. I very much doubt that such a large insect would be a pollinator of this orchid. It was early to see this butterfly on the wing – they are usually a feature of this bushland in late October or early November – but despite the absence of any of its kin it was obviously enjoying the profusion of wildflowers, darting quickly from one blossom to another. This butterfly would have bred on one of the matrushes growing in small unburnt strips along the road. It is remarkable how insects cope with the regular burning of the Australian bush. They survive in small unburnt pockets and then rapidly spread out to recolonise the burnt areas as the food plants shoot again. I remember in the late winter of 1945 following the devastating bushfires at Yallourn in February of the previous year, finding the caterpillars of this same skipper butterfly on the masses of new growth of lomandria; yet it was difficult to find any spot that had escaped the fire. The fresh regrowth seems to be especially attractive to the female butterfly which seeks it out to lay eggs. The rapid resurgence of native insects following fire is also almost certainly favoured by the temporary rarity of parasites, the wasps and flies which prey on the larvae.

A small dragonfly was flying about nearby. It had a very quick and darting flight but was able to halt suddenly in midair and to hover motionless except for the very quick beating of its glistening and transparent wings. And it would then be off again at great speed. What splendid manoeuvrability these creatures have. Yet they possess one of the most primitive wing structures of all those in the insect kingdom and are among the earliest types of insects recorded as fossils.

Later, a pair of much larger dragonflies flew past joined in tandem. I was reminded of the premating performance of dragonflies which is strange

even by insect standards. The male clutches the female just behind the head with two powerful clawlike appendages at the rear of the abdomen and transports her away in nuptial flight. Beforehand, the male transfers sperm from the gonophore at the rear of the abdomen to the penis sac located on the undersurface of the abdomen immediately behind the thorax and its three pairs of legs. To effect copulation, it is necessary for the female dragonfly to curl her abdomen forward in a long loop and attach the female gonophore to the male accessory genitalia.

As I was loading my camera to get the dragonflies on film, I noticed out of the corner of my eye a large, strikingly marked looper caterpillar. It stood out rigidly from the stem of a Gorse Hakea which was equally rigid looking and with very prickly leaves. Posing as a dead twig, its shape was a good imitation but its background yellow colour with black markings and some minute red spots seemed inappropriate. And yet it succeeded in its act of concealment because I had this morning spent a good deal of time next to the bush and it was only now that I had noticed it. As I examined the caterpillar more closely I saw how its markings tended to break up the outline of its body and against a background which included blotches of yellow on the hakea leaves, this brightly coloured looper would

Hairy caterpillar (unidentified).

indeed with a cursory glance be easily missed.

Nearby, a tiger moth caterpillar was flaunting itself on the upright stem of a native grass plant – quite a different strategy to the looper caterpillar. Covered in a dense array of hairs of varying lengths it presumably felt secure in the knowledge that it would prove a most uncomfortable mouthful for any passing bird. However, whilst it seems certain that the hairs do act as a defence against predators, they do appear also to be important sensory organs, sensitive to touch and in some instances sensitive to sounds, causing the caterpillars of some hairy species to freeze instantly in response to low-frequency sound waves.

There were many sun orchids in evidence on this warm and sunny day. They were mostly Rabbits Ears but, as seems common down here, they were not open. The most important factor in determining the opening is temperature. However, humidity is also significant and when humidity is high, a higher temperature is required for the petals to unfold. Generally it is believed that where relative humidity is low, 22 degrees Celsius is sufficient to permit opening but where relative humidity is high, over 25 is required. Given that days of 25 degrees and over are not that common in early and midspring and relative humidity is often high, the flowering season of these orchids is very limited. In fact, a detailed study conducted some years ago at Anglesea showed that the Rabbits Ears Sun Orchid in that particular season (1984) had only 10 hours of suitable weather for opening in 17 days of observation. However, the conditions that favour the opening of the orchid also encourage its pollinators, so opening would be pointless at lower temperatures. Not all the sun orchids are dependent on cross-pollination though, and some rely to a large degree on self-pollination. The Rabbits Ears Orchid, which relies largely on cross-pollination, sets so many seeds from the one flower that even if only a few are pollinated each year, the viability of the local population would still be ensured.

Research work on the Rabbits Ears Orchid strongly suggests that it mimics the flowers of certain other species which it resembles in colour. Several plants may be involved but the two most important here are a species of guinea flower and a yellow-flowering goodenia. These flowers are much commoner than Rabbits Ears and by opening during the flowering period of the other plants the orchid is able to cash in on the insects which pollinate those species. The Rabbits Ears offer no rewards to insect visitors – a native bee (*Lasioglossum*) and a cosmopolitan hoverfly – but nevertheless they have been found with the orchid's pollinia attached to them. Such 'deceitful' mimicry requires that the orchid mimic be relatively rare compared to the models, the guinea flowers and the goodenia, otherwise the pollinators would quickly learn of the deception and ignore the orchid.

TOP: Rabbits Ears Orchids (Thelymitra antennifera).

BOTTOM: A morel (Morchella elata)—*a prized edible fungus.*

22 OCTOBER

The weather prospects looked excellent when I left home this morning at six. I parked my car at the first parking spot before Point Addis and made my way down the steep cliff to the beach.

There has been a big rockfall on the northern side of Point Addis since my last visit. Huge boulders weighing many tonnes have fallen out of the cliff onto the beach on the northeast side of the point. These falls result from the undermining of the cliff profile by water seeping down from higher layers.

I found a number of small sea urchins washed up on the beach. Some were quite fresh with the spines intact and with marked striations radiating out from the apex. I wonder why they should appear at this time. I have not seen them here before. Have they been washed in by a recent storm or have they migrated to the rear of the shore platform and been left stranded at the low tide? An interesting feature of sea urchins – which are nearly always seen in the form of the old shell rather than the living creature – is that in live specimens the spines are covered by an almost invisible skin. The spines rotate individually on joints and by means of muscles can move in any direction. The spines and the tube feet, like those of the starfish, can be extended outward to provide a grip on a smooth rock surface enabling sea urchins to move easily across the floor and walls of rock pools.

The low tide had exposed multicoloured limpets on the rocks. The radiating

ABOVE: *Sea urchin*
(Heliocidaris
erythrogramma*).*

RIGHT: *Early morning, Addiscott
Beach.*

bands of colour on these shells are most attractive, particularly as individuals in any group are likely to exhibit different shades and patterns. Limpets belong to the family Patellidae. Although they give every appearance of being permanently fixed to one point on the rock surface, they are in fact quite mobile and at high tide they move away to forage on seaweed, always returning to the same indentation on the rock surface. The most common limpet species here (*Cellana tramoserica*) accounts for a high proportion of old shells found on beaches along this coast. This species was an important component of the Aborigines' shellfish diet as can be seen by the huge number of these shells found on the middens.

25 OCTOBER

I have been planning for some time to visit some 'big trees' located on the West Barham River, near Apollo Bay. An opportunity came up today and a group of us led by local ranger Paul Millar set out at 9.30 am to explore this interesting area.

Under Paul's guidance we headed due west from the road directly up a very steep incline. Ducking under tree ferns, sliding over mossy fallen logs and slipping in places on muddy, sloping stretches, we made it to the top of the first ridge where the country fortunately opened up somewhat. There were large Messmates and a few Mountain Ash with hazel and

LEFT: Tree ferns and distant Mountain Ash (Eucalyptus regnans).

BELOW: Unfolding fronds, Soft Tree Fern (Dicksonia antarctica).

Low tide, Urquhart Bluff.

Satinwood as understorey. As we descended downhill along a ridge towards the West Barham River we veered southwest passing a few white-trunked trees we thought were probably Mountain Grey Gum. A little beyond this point we reconnoitred to consider our position against a map and compass. Because the country looked unfamiliar to Paul who had been here before, our best bet seemed to be to strike directly down to the river and traverse it first one way then the other until we could see the big trees. This we did and after one false sortie upriver, eventually arrived at the big trees at 1.30 pm, some four hours after setting out! In this country, with visibility reduced in most situations to less than 100 metres, and with gullies and ridges running in all directions, it is very easy indeed to get off course even with the aid of a compass.

The West Barham is a small, clear, fast-flowing stream. There was very little evidence of weeds or of any previous visitation by people and it was a very tranquil setting with the sun shining through huge tree ferns, Blackwoods and the occasional ancient Myrtle Beech. One rough tree fern we found was over three metres around the butt and it would have been almost eight metres high.

We also located a very large Myrtle Beech over 30 metres high and a metre or more in diameter and it was strangely isolated. I wondered if it was a survivor from a fire that swept down the bed of this river many years ago.

At one point on the bank above the river and above the level of the tree ferns we watched a Rufous Fantail swooping and in some instances successfully catching what appeared to be midges or perhaps small craneflies above the tree fern canopy.

There were few opportunities to take photographs of the river scenery. We had to keep moving and sudden bursts of wind funnelling through the narrow gully of the West Barham kept the fern fronds swaying. Without still conditions in a low-light environment such as this one, it is not possible to stop down the lens sufficiently to obtain the desirable depth of focus. I did manage a few shots but I was not happy that they would produce good results.

The sight of the big trees was enthralling, many probably approaching 90 metres in height, although in most instances broken at the top. Some had been badly damaged by wind storms. The largest trees were on a ridge and exposed to the full force of the elements and not surprisingly these were the worst affected. We also noticed ancient fire scars on different sides of the trees and hence probably not from the same fire. The scars showed no sign of charcoal so they must have been from very old fires. I wondered if these trees had survived the famous 1851 fire which swept through this area when it burnt out the then tiny settlement of Apollo Bay.

It was noticeable that below some of the undamaged and taller trees there was no sign of fallen limbs. The process of decay here must be very slow since the trees are estimated to be 300 years old or more. However, judging by their appearance, they reach a certain stage of growth and then deteriorate more quickly.

Against one of the trees I photographed, six of our party could stand comfortably in a row in front of the buttresses at the base. The first limb did not appear for 46 metres above their heads. But as always, photographing these trees is extremely difficult and even with a wide-angle lens it is not possible to get far enough away to convey the true impression of their size. I found a few leaves on the ground presumably blown from the uppermost branches in a recent storm. They were surprisingly small, about eight centimetres long and considerably smaller than the leaves of young Mountain Ash which are around 20 centimetres long in its spar stage at around 40 years of age. As Mountain Ash approaches maturity at 150 years, growth slows down and, as a consequence one imagines, of their immense height above the ground and the difficulty of drawing water and nutrients up from the roots, the uppermost leaves become smaller and thickened. The uppermost leaves, too, are fully exposed to the elements and have to survive in a much harsher and less protected environment than those at lower heights.

NOVEMBER

LEFT: Spring sunrise, Addiscott Beach.

ABOVE: Pied Oystercatcher.

4 NOVEMBER

Today I decided to include a visit to Ocean Grove. The township is somewhat outside the area I have been studying, being about 20 kilometres east of Bells Beach, the most easterly visiting spot I had chosen. The Ocean Grove district encompasses one quite different vegetation type and has some natural history interest which I believe could add to my Otway story.

My first destination was a patch of remnant bushland, northeast of Ocean Grove, now surrounded by houses, factories and cleared farmland. I remember it over 40 years ago when I used to search for hours among the Yellow Gums, Silver Banksias and the Golden Wattles for the caterpillars and pupae of the Small Ant Blue and the Fiery Jewel butterflies. Both are associated with small brown ants which have no common name but the forbidding Latin title of *Iridomyrmex nitidus*. It is a species which builds nests in tree stumps, fallen logs, old fence posts and under bark. The ant readily reveals its presence by the layers of small leaves and other plant debris it places on top of the nest and, if examined more closely, by the characteristic and not unattractive coconutlike smell emitted when it is disturbed. One assumes this odour must be distasteful to its natural predators.

The ants in the case of both butterfly species attend the larvae. With the Small Ant Blue there is no evidence that the larvae eat plant material. The Fiery Jewel larvae on the other hand crawl up the trunk of the Golden Wattles to feed on the leaves at night. They eat them in a very singular manner, signs of their nightly forages, if there are enough of them, being fairly obvious by the burnt appearance of the phyllodes. During the day they live at the base of the wattle.

The Small Ant Blue larvae, however, seemingly never leave the ants' nest and if removed from the ant byre, disdain any samples of the surrounding vegetation offered them. It would be extremely difficult to simulate artificially the conditions of the ants' nest and to breed this butterfly away from the very special environment in which it lives. To my knowledge, nobody has yet proved what seems to be the only explanation of its life history, namely that the butterfly caterpillars eat the larvae and pupae of the ants that attend them. Such a bizarre relationship has been established for the English Ant Blue and it seems highly likely that our own species enjoys the same curious relationship with its hosts.

Female Small Ant Blue butterfly (Acrodipsas myrmecophila) *recently emerged from chrysalis.*

It is now generally believed that the larvae of many blue butterflies secrete not only a sugary solution, much prized by the attending ants, but also a pheromone, or scent, produced in minute quantities and which closely resembles that produced by the ants' own larvae. It is thought that the pheromone tends to control the ants' natural aggression and in this case presumably allows the Ant Blue caterpillar to roam at will in the ants' nest and to feed without apparent retaliation by the ants on their own larvae and pupae.

Curious as this relationship may seem, it pales into insignificance compared with another of the blue butterflies called the Moth butterfly from North Queensland. This species also occurs throughout Papua New Guinea, Indonesia, Malaysia and India. The life history was elucidated many years ago by the famous 'butterfly man', Frank Dodd of Kuranda, North Queensland. It includes a larval period in which the insect living in the nest of the Greentree Ant, a very pugnacious and stinging creature, eats the ants' larvae but is protected from the ravages of this ferocious ant by a shell-like cuticle which prevents them inflicting any wounds on the soft caterpillar inside. Presumably to provide shelter at a very vulnerable stage, it pupates within its final larval skin so the ants are unable to attack it in this immobile state. The larva remains for some time in the nest as a fully protected pupa. On emergence, the limp and as yet unexpanded butterfly is covered in easily removed white scales which attach themselves to the attacking Greentree Ants who are soon immobilised, allowing the butterfly to escape and to expand its wings and eventually fly away.

Knowing the area so well from years ago, I was keen today to see if the Ant Blue was still here. The Fiery Jewel is best sought later in the season. Although I searched for more than an hour, I could find no nests at all, let alone the nest of the Small Ant Blue. Forty years ago ant nests were so common that it often took hours to find a nest with any Ant Blue larvae in it, even though the butterfly was then undoubtedly quite common. But the ants have either completely disappeared or are now very rare. Why?

The answer almost certainly lies in subtle changes to the environment. The vegetation has not been cleared but it has grown denser and weeds of various sorts have invaded both the upper storey and the understorey of this low scrub. There is now less light penetrating the low canopy because

the Golden Wattles have proliferated but more importantly because the Coast Tea Tree has run wild. Although not native to this particular locality, it has succeeded in dominating much of the reserve with its denser foliage. Other alien plants occurring in patches, particularly on the outskirts, are smilax, gorse and pines.

Later on during the day on the path to Teddys Lookout above Lorne, which yields splendid views of the winding Ocean Road and of the rugged Otway coastline, I encountered an insect sometimes called the Blue Ant (*Diamma bicolor*). It is wingless and holds its abdomen in an upright and threatening manner and moves actively over the ground rather like a highly metallic blue version of a bullant. In fact it is a member of the family of flower wasps (Thynnidae) and is unusual in that most female wasps in this family are much smaller than the male who transports the female to flowers to feed her and later to copulate. The male then carries the female to the breeding ground where hopefully she will locate suitable larvae beneath the ground, usually of scarab beetles, on which to lay her eggs. The Blue Ant, however, is a parasite of mole crickets and is said to possess a particularly painful sting.

8 NOVEMBER

This morning I walked to the rock pool at Urquhart Bluff. The tide was coming in and there was just room to get around the point without getting myself and the cameras wet. The rock pool itself was well filled and the water was extraordinarily clear, even though it is a couple of metres deep in the middle. Rock pools such as this provide a very dynamic environment as conditions vary continually during the day, mainly due to the influence of tides.

There was the usual accumulation of shells on the edge of the pool. One yellow cowrie shell I photographed was neatly marked with two darker transverse bands running across it. Cowries are not particularly common here but you can usually find a few old shells about. These shells are much better developed in the tropics where there is a great range of species, some of which are large and beautifully patterned. The secret of the cowrie's highly polished shell lies in the fact that the mantle of the living cowrie extends out and around the shell, fully enveloping and protecting it. Only in relatively old shells does this highly enamelled sheen disappear. The other feature which distinguishes cowries from other shells is the long narrow mouth, or opening, and the teeth or grooves which lie along it.

Another striking shell I photographed was a pink and mauve cone shell. As with the cowries, cone shells attain their greatest diversity, size and beauty in the tropics, although a few species do appear in temperate waters. Some cone shells are capable of poisoning those who handle living specimens carelessly, although I think only tropical species have been implicated in fatalities. The teeth of the living cone shell have glands which, in some species, secrete a highly virulent poison. The cone shell differs from other shellfish in the mobility of its mouthparts, which can be extended or retracted very quickly to attack its prey or defend itself from a predator.

Despite this small treasure-trove, shells are relatively uncommon here, even though the shore platforms of this coast would seem to be ideal for molluscs. But walking back along the sand nearer the car park I picked up a handsome bivalve shell with an enamelled purple inner surface. You see fewer intact bivalve shells on the shore platforms, possibly because they are destroyed by wave action, being brushed against the hard resistant rock.

ABOVE: Cone shell (Conus anemone).

BELOW: Rock pool shells, Urquhart Bluff, cowrie (Cypraea comptoni)*, pheasant shells* (Phasianella australis).

10 NOVEMBER

ABOVE: *A cave near Cinema Point.*

BELOW: *A flower of Blue Pincushion* (Brunonia australis).

This morning I headed directly to Eastern View, a few kilometres southwest of Aireys Inlet. Geologically it is an interesting area where the older Cretaceous sediments making up the bulk of the Otways first appear as you journey down the Great Ocean Road.

My aim this morning was to explore this rugged section of coastline. The timing was ideal because, not only was the weather excellent, but low tide was predicted for 7.15 am at Port Phillip Heads 30 kilometres to the northeast. I was scrambling over the masses of fallen rocks which lie at the foot of the cliffs near Cinema Point before seven.

As with so much of the exposed sandstone along this coastline, the boulders here are frequently honeycombed from weathering by wind and sea water. There were many excellent collections of rocks of different colours, shapes and textures, but rather than photograph them in what would have been an excellent soft early morning light, I made directly for a big cave which is said to have been used by William Buckley. He was a convict who escaped from Captain Collins's abortive attempt at settlement near Sorrento in 1803. Unlike his companions, he was not recaptured. He reappeared some 30 years later when John Batman led his band of settlers to Port Phillip Bay from Tasmania. Buckley's story of his lost 32 years has never been thoroughly pieced together, partly because he seems perhaps understandably not to have been very articulate. Buckley apparently lived with Aborigines based near Geelong and eventually adopted their life style, so much so that he temporarily lost the use of his native English tongue. In the days and weeks following his escape, Buckley travelled along the southwest coastline, apparently reaching as far as Mount Defiance. He kept alive on a diet of shellfish which were plentiful on the coast and an important component of the diet of the local Aborigines.

Several caves are claimed to have been used by Buckley, most notably one at Point Lonsdale. The Cinema Point cave is likely to have at least been a temporary haven for Buckley, because it is ideally situated high above even the biggest waves and protected from the southwesterly winds by a massive rock barrier in front of the cave mouth. It would be a comfortable place to rest and, because the floor is evenly covered with a deep layer of fine sand, it would be soft.

I decided to spend the rest of the day covering a broad sweep of the Anglesea heath catching some of the late spring flowering plants. The road I was following winds down through the heathland to the valley of Salt Creek, a tributary of the Anglesea River, before becoming the Bald Hills Road. Salt Creek, an extremely sluggish stream which seems to be more

FAR LEFT: Swordgrass Brown butterfly (Tisiphone abeona albifascia*).*

LEFT: Eyespots on hindwings of the Ringed Xenica butterfly (Geitoneura acantha ocrea*).*

an extended marsh, is very different from the surrounding sandy country and contains a number of interesting plant species. One of these is the Running Marsh Flower, a bright yellow-flowering plant which grows in water, often among rushes.

There is also an interesting range of vegetation here from woodland dominated by Messmate to quite dense thickets of Prickly Moses and open patches of heath. It is the type of country I would like to visit later in the year, particularly with a light at night to sample the insect life. It appears to have more variation than other parts of the Anglesea heathland.

On the way back along the track I saw a large, freshly emerged specimen of the Swordgrass Brown butterfly. It was almost black and with broad orange bars on the forewing and red and blue coloured eyespots this insect is an unmistakable sight in the bush. It wended its way with ease through the thickets of Prickly Moses and was soon gone, its seemingly slow flight belying its great manoeuvrability in such dense undergrowth. I imagine there must be occasions when they are caught by birds. Yet it is a species whose wings I have not yet seen on tracks where Willy Wagtails, notorious insect-feeding birds, leave the remains of their feasts. Maybe its huge eyespots act as a distraction to birds. It is claimed birds pick at the false eyes or ocelli on the wings of butterflies and moths like these and so miss the vital parts.

The Swordgrass Brown is one of Australia's most intriguing butterflies. Over its range from Gympie in Queensland down the eastern coast to the far west of South Australia, it has developed no less than seven races or subspecies. The four northern races, where the black is offset with white markings, are strikingly different from the three southern subspecies which have a large orange band on the forewing as their predominant distinguishing feature. It is thought that the southern and northern forms must have been separated by a substantial physical barrier for a long period for such a distinctive difference to develop. They now meet near Port Macquarie in New South Wales to form a very variable population with a range of forms intermediate between the two basic orange and white groups of the butterfly.

The development of such races or subspecies is controlled by two opposing forces: selection which operates in isolation, and dispersal which occurs in the absence of physical barriers to reduce local variation occurring within a species.

The Swordgrass Brown in the Otways might be expected to differ from the albifascia form which occupies eastern Victoria and southeastern New South Wales, but in fact it appears to be all but identical; this despite the development in the Otways of racial characteristics in other 'brown' butterflies inherently less variable than the Swordgrass Brown. The brown butterflies of the Otways have presumably been isolated by the basalt lava flows of western Victoria. These flows cut off the Otways from comparable areas of vegetation in eastern Victoria.

How has the Swordgrass Brown butterfly avoided this effect of isolation? It seems unlikely that in recent times there was a connecting corridor of its food plant, the Red Fruit Sawsedge, which requires damp conditions to flourish, across the relatively dry volcanic plains between the Otways and the Central Highlands. Is it possible that odd individuals have blown in from the Eastern Highlands across the sea from, say, Arthur's Seat where it occurs? Such enforced and occasional flights of odd individuals might account for why this butterfly has failed to respond to the isolation of the Otways.

The weather by one o'clock today had begun to turn cloudy; there were a few spots of rain and the forecast was beginning to look quite accurate! I took time to examine, between short bursts of sunshine, a low peak overlooking the Alcoa brown-coal mine and a hill that I have not examined before. Looking down into the open-cut, the dark brown coal layers are obvious. Above them is a light-coloured portion of the profile which includes clay layers containing plant fossils.

At least two separate plant communities are represented by these fossils. One dominated by a cycad related to the she-oaks which can still be found here, and the other a subtropical rainforest with over 100 plant species identified. It seems incredible that some 20 metres below the present-day heathland are the fossilised remains of a rainforest. Yet in that period, the late Eocene some 35 million years ago, before Australia began to separate from Antarctica, the climate was warm and humid. After separation, cold currents began to flow along the newly formed southern coastline and the climate is believed to have become much colder and drier. The rainforests retreated northward and became extinct in the Anglesea area. Among the rainforest fossils are examples of the family Proteacea, still well represented today in the Anglesea heathland in the form of banksias, hakeas and geebungs.

Coast Beard Heath
(Leucopogon parviflorus).

13 NOVEMBER

In the cooler high rainfall areas near Weeaproinah on the Otway Ridge at 500 metres elevation, the country remains lush and green. The vegetation and scenery are reminiscent of the dune country at Yanakie, just north of Wilsons Promontory. I noted a few bushes of smilax, a pink-flowered weed which is a nuisance in the coastal scrub on the Mornington Peninsula. It is a garden escapee like so many of our brightly coloured weeds.

There is an abundance of Coast Tea Tree at Cape Otway, particularly on the dunes just behind the lighthouse. Was this planted and if so, when? It is claimed that this species did not occur naturally southwest of Torquay, but since it is growing so enthusiastically down here now it is hard to see why it would not have found its way down the coastline thousands of years ago. Growing with the tea tree were two plants which undoubtedly

Caper White butterfly
(Anaphaeis java teutonia).

have always occurred here: Coast Beard Heath and Silver Banksia.

I saw a few Caper White butterflies in seemingly aimless flight. Have these butterflies become detached from one of the big migratory flights they make from time to time in eastern Australia? The reason why Caper Whites migrate in huge numbers remains a mystery. They breed in northern New South Wales and southern Queensland inland from the coast where the larvae feed on various species of capers. They fly away from their breeding ground for no apparent reason – males and females in equal numbers – and make no effort to breed en route even where their food plant is available. Since caper plants do not extend south of northern New South Wales and there is no alternative food plant for the larvae, their flights seem to be totally without purpose. Sometimes the flights occur on vast fronts many kilometres in width and may continue for days on end. In their southward migrations, Caper Whites have been known to reach Tasmania, but the vast majority that fly south of the mainland perish in the ocean, their bodies later lining the beaches of the southern coast.

One butterfly I found seemed very tired. Usually they are constantly on the move, but this one fluttered over the grass in short bursts and was content to settle on twigs. I wondered if the long flight it must have made from northern inland New South Wales or southern Queensland could have exhausted its supplies of energy. This would represent about the last landfall the insect would have on a southern flight and the furthest distance they can fly overland in their strange migratory flights. In any event, its lack of activity proved a boon to me and I was able to take a close-up photograph of this individual, something that has eluded me in the last few weeks, although I have seen many of them.

With the prospect of better weather I made my way from Lavers Hill and then on to Gibsons Steps a few kilometres east of Princetown. The view from the top of the steps looking west towards the Twelve Apostles is very striking although difficult to photograph in the late afternoon as I was looking almost directly into the sun. The name Twelve Apostles seems strange to me since I could see only nine of these small islands and there is no record of three disappearing. However, I am told that it depends on what you include in the count and some of the more distant islands were presumably outside my view. Their biblical title replaced an even less appropriate name of the Sow and Piglets!

*ABOVE: Coral fern (Gleichenia
sp), Carlisle Heath.*

*BELOW: Damsel fly
(Austrolestes leda).*

17 & 18 NOVEMBER

Taking the dirt road from Gellibrand to Carlisle early this morning, I stopped at a damp patch of bushland between five and 10 kilometres west of the township. The weather conditions were very dull and cool with the ever-present threat of rain.

I noted the penetrating smell of Shining Peppermint. As with all the peppermints, damp air following rain seems to accentuate this powerful aroma, which to my nose is most attractive. The area here at Carlisle is said to be the best representative of this type of heathy woodlands dominated by Shining Peppermint and subject to considerably higher rainfall than the heathy woodlands near Anglesea. The understorey is well endowed with Silky Tea Tree now at the height of its flowering with cascades of attractive white symmetrical flowers but almost entirely without insect visitors. I did see a sole large black ant examining one of the blossoms, but nothing more.

A few kilometres into the Carlisle Park I spied an old dirt track paralleling the road I was on but further down the valley. My first discovery on clambering down to the road was a damsel fly which I inadvertently disturbed from its perch on a tea tree branch. It soon obliged, however, by resettling on a dead eucalypt nearby. I have noted with a similar species in my garden in Melbourne that, when settling, these flies move their long, fine, pointed abdomens upwards and downwards half a dozen times like a wagging finger before adopting the typical rigid resting pose with the body held at an angle of about 45 degrees to the horizontal. Damsel flies are clearly distinguishable from their relatives, the dragonflies, because as well as having a much more delicate structure, they settle with their wings closed. Most often the wings are transparent and it was a delicacy of the reflected rainbow colours that I hoped to catch today in my photographs. The complex pattern of the veins of damsel flies and the wings also caught my eye. The veins and subveins box in tiny areas to form vast numbers of cells in each wing.

Like dragonflies, damsel flies are primarily aquatic with the immature or nymphal stages usually living in water or predominantly damp areas. Both the nymph and the adult are carnivorous; the former stalking or lying in wait for waterborne prey, the latter catching flying insects in their spiny, rapacious-looking forelegs.

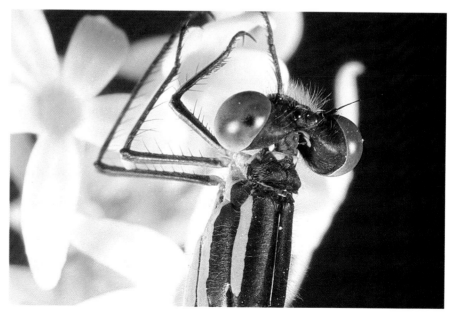

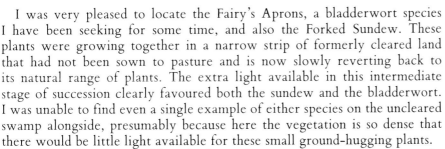

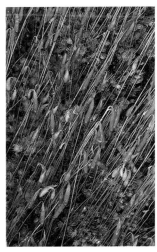

I was very pleased to locate the Fairy's Aprons, a bladderwort species
I have been seeking for some time, and also the Forked Sundew. These
plants were growing together in a narrow strip of formerly cleared land
that had not been sown to pasture and is now slowly reverting back to
its natural range of plants. The extra light available in this intermediate
stage of succession clearly favoured both the sundew and the bladderwort.
I was unable to find even a single example of either species on the uncleared
swamp alongside, presumably because here the vegetation is so dense that
there would be little light available for these small ground-hugging plants.

The Fairy's Aprons, although they rely on waterborne insects caught
in bladders below the ground for food, are not strictly aquatic plants. They
always live, however, in a permanently moist environment and below ground
level the bladders catch living organisms such as daphnia. After photographing
one of the few specimens in flower – it has a deep violet flower consisting
of two petals, one larger and more triangular in shape and forming the
apron, and the other, a smaller upright petal – I extracted the whole plant
carefully from the peat in which it was growing. I washed the soil away
carefully in a small pond. A mass of white almost translucent 'roots' was
revealed and I laid these out on the surface of the bare black peat to provide
the best possible contrast to highlight the tiny bladders. They were not

RIGHT: *Underground stems and single bladder of Fairy's Aprons* (Utricularia dichotoma).

FAR RIGHT: *The Forked Sundew* (Drosera binata).

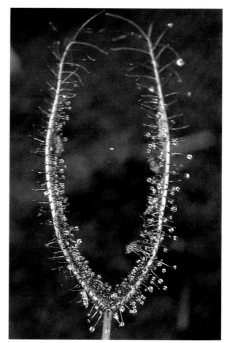

as obvious as I had hoped but I found what I believe to be one, more or less spherical in shape.

The bladderworts do not have roots in the normal sense of the word. The white hairlike growths I examined were in fact elongated stems from which the leaves develop. In this species a rosette of leaves forms around the stem at ground level. The essential feature of these plants is the unique bladder. In these subterranean organs, prey is trapped to supplement the plant's supply of nutrients in a fashion analogous to the insect-catching behaviour of sundews. The traps of the bladderwort are very intricate and specialised. A 'hinged' trapdoor covers the entrance to the bladder. The door remains shut through a finely balanced tension between the suction caused by a partial vacuum in the bladder and the 'spring' of the door. Long, sensitive hairs attached to the edge of the trapdoor act as levers and if touched by a passing insect immediately trigger the opening of the door. The trapped insect eventually dies and is digested by enzymes secreted by glands within the bladder. Water is gradually removed from the bladder by other specialised glands and the partial vacuum is restored.

The whole action of entrapping the prey is said to take between 10 and 15 thousandths of a second. The reverse movement of water out of the bladder to restore the vacuum is a much slower process. Two hours later the desirable low pressure has been reached and the outer surface of the bladder assumes a concave appearance and is then primed ready for the next victim.

The action of the neighbouring Forked Sundews was much easier to see and to comprehend. The fork of these sundews is very like a tuning fork, each prong arising from a single junction. They were covered with masses of bristled, sticky glands and in several cases were heavily loaded with small insects, nearly all of them flies. The insects will be digested in time to supplement the dietary requirements of the sundew. Both of these botanically unrelated plants, the bladderwort and the sundew, are making use of nutrient supplementation in a soil where the anaerobic conditions make life difficult for other pioneering plants.

On my way to Anglesea to photograph some Potato Orchids I saw a Black Wallaby feeding on grass on the roadside. You can often approach them closely in a car but I have noted the ones here are particularly tame, presumably because they have been used to fairly frequent traffic. This wallaby remained with its head buried in the low roadside vegetation for long periods; with its curved back, black tail and long head, it looked like some strange, semicircular black object. I approached a point where I could take some effective photographs with a long-focal-length lens and a tripod. It looked up surprised and I guess fearful, revealing the soft light brown colour of its neck below the head and its alert twitching ears and ever watchful eyes. I pushed the camera shutter very carefully but it heard the sound from 40 metres because it immediately hopped away.

Unfortunately, the Potato Orchids had finished flowering. Their short flowering period has probably been encouraged by the recent spell of very hot weather. This was a disappointment because I would have liked to photograph the species here where they occur as a smaller version of the ones I am familiar with in the higher rainfall country east of Melbourne.

The Potato Orchid, like the Hyacinth Orchid, has no leaves and its light brown stem and flower stalks contain very little chlorophyll. Thus, unlike other plants, the Potato Orchid is unable to rely on photosynthesis for its supply of carbohydrates and instead depends on an association with mycorrhizal fungi in the soil.

Given the very specific soil and climate requirements and fungal association of the Potato Orchid, it is remarkable that it has become established in South Africa following accidental introduction near Cape Town in 1944. Presumably the Potato Orchid gained entry as seed or as tubers in samples of soil surrounding imported Australian eucalypt seedlings. But the orchid invasion has not been in one direction and slightly earlier than 1944 a South African orchid (*Monadenia bracteata*) was noted in Albany and has since established itself more widely in southwestern Australia. How it arrived remains a mystery.

Although the Potato Orchids were disappointing, I decided to have a look for some Small Duck Orchids that might have opened by now. Last week when I looked for them I could only find specimens in bud. I soon located a group in flower and as I prepared to take a very close range photograph of one, I must have touched it because the head snapped down and instantly the flying duck look had gone! With a little more patience and care I was more successful with a second open orchid.

What strikes you when looking at these small orchids, other than their resemblance to a duck, is the labellum or tongue covered with very dark tubercles looking like so many black clubs. Research on a very closely allied

FAR LEFT: *The Potato Orchid* (Gastrodia sesamoides).

LEFT: *Little Duck Orchid* (Paracaleana minor).

205

duck orchid from Western Australia has revealed a most unusual and highly specific pollination mechanism involving a small species of thynnid wasp with a winged male and wingless female. The habit of the female is to sit on a flower to await the arrival of the male which she grabs and then is transported away and mates. On visiting the orchid the male wasp mistakenly alights on the part of the orchid which to us resembles the head of a duck but to the wasp it is a female of its own species. Propelled by the weight of the male wasp the 'head' moves down and triggers a trapping mechanism which snares the wasp in close proximity to the orchid's pollen-bearing organs. Eventually it struggles free but not before the orchid's pollen is transferred to it.

23 NOVEMBER

Each burst of sunshine today brought out a mass of flying insects, most seeking nectar and pollen from the many wildflowers still in bloom. I noted native bees, wasps, dragonflies, day-flying moths, grasshoppers and butterflies.

Several skipper butterflies flew swiftly along the bush track where I was walking – the Donnysa, the Phigalia, and the Phigaloides. All had the typically fast jerky flight of skippers. They were males, each defending its territory and hoping to find a mate. The females, less aggressive and demonstrative, are more likely to be found on flowers or seeking out food plants on which to lay their eggs.

One settled close to my feet. It was a male Phigaloides Skipper, and was soon challenged by another male. It took off in fast spiralling chase that I could only follow for a second or two, then disappeared. Half a minute later it reappeared as if from nowhere to land in exactly the same spot on the track, having presumably frightened away its rival.

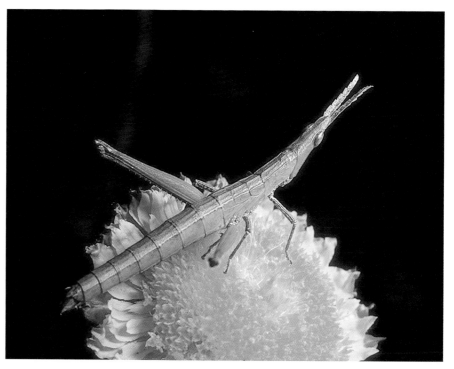

Grasshopper (Morabinae) on an everlasting flower (Helichrysum sp).

LEFT: *Hairy Flower wasp (Scoliidae) on everlasting (Helichrysum sp).*

ABOVE: *A Donnysa Skipper (Hesperilla donnysa delos) on a flower of an everlasting (Helichrysum sp).*

BELOW: *A forester moth (Pollanisus viridipulverulenta) sucking nectar from a flower of an everlasting (Helichrysum sp).*

Skipper butterflies have very stout muscular bodies. Because of their small size, the speed and erratic nature of their flight and drab colour, they are not often noticed by the bushwalker or naturalist. With their curiously recurved, clubbed antennae and dull colouring they might easily be mistaken for moths.

I was delighted to find an uncommon and beautiful orchid, the Blotched Sun Orchid. Sun orchids, as the name suggests, mostly display their flowers in warm, sunny weather and remain closed on cool, cloudy days. Spring weather, particularly in these parts, is so often cool and cloudy that you can make several visits to the one site yet never find a sun orchid open.

Sun orchids are unusually regular, almost symmetrical in shape when compared with other orchids. The tongue, or labellum, often a spectacular and distinguishing feature of other orchids, in the sun orchid is shaped and

ABOVE: *Blotched Sun Orchid* (Thelymitra benthamiana).

RIGHT: *The column of the Great Sun Orchid* (Thelymitra aristata).

coloured very much like the other petals, which technically speaking it is anyway. The column containing the reproductive parts is relatively small – a few millimetres in height. Only when you examine it closely, preferably with a hand lens, do you appreciate the intricate and often beautiful structure. It almost seems that much of the character and individuality of sun orchids has been condensed into the tiny column, the larger petals and sepals of quite different species often being surprisingly similar in shape and colour.

A pair of copulating scorpion flies flew slowly past in the light breeze as I walked down the track. Eventually they settled on a small bush and I was able to photograph them. What I saw intrigued me. One of the scorpion flies was holding a small fly, a little bigger than a house fly, which it had apparently captured earlier and anaesthetised.

The love life of scorpion flies, which belong to the very ancient insect order Mecoptera, is both complicated and bizarre. After capturing its insect prey, the male transfers its catch to its hindlegs and waits for a female. The female, which is said to be attracted by a musky secretion, is grabbed by the male and copulation commences. At the same time the male transfers its prey to the female, who proceeds to feed on it. After the female has finished feeding, she flies away, leaving the male to finish the meal. Only a scorpion fly that has captured an insect is attractive to the female, although the male can mate with more than one female using the same prey. It is believed that the female needs the food in order to ensure the maturation of her eggs. The larvae of scorpion flies feed on dead insects and pupate below the surface of the ground.

There were very few birds on the wing today, and only magpies and Crimson Rosellas made any impression on me as I concentrated on the low understorey of flowering plants.

Many trees appear to be dying. Some are already dead, gaunt grey skeletons in a naturally sparse woodland. They are almost certainly infested with a fungal parasite, *Phytopthora cinnamomi*, known commonly as dieback. It is a disease for which there is still no practical cure and which endangers the future of this unique botanical association.

It is now generally agreed that dieback was introduced into Australia last century. It probably came in soil associated with imported plant specimens. The disease is rife in the jarrah forests of Western Australia and is an increasing problem in the eastern States. In Victoria it threatens valuable timber resources in East Gippsland and national parks at Wilsons Promontory and the Brisbane Ranges.

Dieback infects over 400 different species of plants, many of them Australian natives, and its effect on bushland in susceptible areas can be devastating. Banksias, heaths, guinea flowers and cone bushes all succumb to the disease, as well as the more obvious eucalypts.

Dieback invades new areas by the spreading of gravel from infected areas onto forest roads or on the blades and tracks of bulldozers which have been working in dieback forests. Once established, it spreads rapidly and its advance in the Brisbane Ranges on drainage slopes has been measured at over 100 metres per year. It proliferates by means of tiny spores known as zoo-spores, which move freely in water and affect the roots of trees and shrubs. Mycelium from zoo-spores invades the root tissues and reduces the plants' ability to take up water. Thus dieback flourishes on shallow, poorly drained soils with an impervious layer close to the surface. Such ground provides a waterlogged environment during the wetter months that allows the disease to spread, and it dries out rapidly in summer, subjecting susceptible plants with weakened root systems to desiccation. An additional factor in these poorly drained soils is their very low inherent fertility with low populations of microorganisms, where the dieback fungus faces a minimum of competition.

Control of the disease currently centres on limiting its spread by adequate hygiene: the thorough washing-down of vehicles working in infected areas before they are released to clean areas, and to close monitoring of the spreading of road gravel.

Some native shrubs are particularly sensitive to dieback and very quickly indicate the presence of the parasite. One such plant is the grass tree and several here were in an advanced state of decay. The typically blackened trunks displayed a few dead leaves trailing sadly onto the ground and nearby were disintegrating trunks with broken pieces strewn around.

DECEMBER

LEFT: Deeply incised meanders on the lower reaches of the Johanna River.

ABOVE: Pale Flax Lily flower (Dianella longifolia), Carlisle Heathland.

A spider (Eriophora *sp*)
captures a feather.

1&2 DECEMBER

My destination this morning was the Cumberland River, a few kilometres southwest of Lorne. The trip down was uneventful with cloudy conditions and intermittent bursts of sunshine.

The river is now very swollen and has obviously flooded in the last few days. The entrance road was not accessible with water running too deeply over the concrete ford to permit vehicle traffic.

I walked up river to Jebbs Pool where I spent the afternoon photographing the patterns of the lichens on the broad and flat expanses of rock alongside the waterfall. It is dry at the mouth and easy to get to; as a result many of the lichen displays have been walked on and spoiled by visitors. I managed to find some undamaged specimens on the edge of the rock as it runs down steeply to the deep pool below the falls.

With crustose forms of lichen it is common to find several species or different colour forms of the same species growing together, and striking coloured patterns result. Crustose lichens adhere very closely to the surface of the rock or bark on which they rest. When a vertical section is examined under the microscope, a complex structure is revealed in the often less than one-millimetre thickness of lichen 'skin' covering the rock surface. There are three parts to this composite organism. The fungal component of this composite plant provides the basic structure, the medulla on which rests an algal layer, the whole organism being covered by what is known as a cortex.

Sometimes crustose lichens are highly specific, occurring only on certain rocks or on the bark of a particular tree. Others are less demanding and are found on a variety of substrates. On exposed rocks, crustose lichens must endure great variation of temperature and even in the relatively mild climate of the Otways it could range from below freezing in winter to well over 40 degrees Celsius on an exposed surface on a hot summer's day. In more extreme climates, lichens have survived on rock surfaces which have reached 65 degrees Celsius and have recovered from temperatures as low as minus 150 degrees Celsius. Lichens, unlike flowering plants, are able to endure total desiccation.

Late in the afternoon I climbed the cliffs on a northeastern bank of the estuary of the Cumberland River, aiming to scale the high point several hundred metres directly above the camping area. There appears to be some form of structure up there, perhaps a lookout, but I could find no obvious way of getting to it.

Visitors have obviously made their way up the steep slopes above the Ocean Road. I followed one track until it petered out in some dense undergrowth of Large-leafed Bushpea, an attractive plant with predominantly yellow flowers with red markings and closely bunched flowering heads at the end of long branches. It seems to prefer the dry northern slopes and has undoubtedly proliferated as a result of fire, the effects of which could readily be seen on the few straggly Messmates growing at intervals on the slopes. Both wallabies and rabbits have clearly been moving through the thickets here. The ground underfoot was virtually bare because so little light penetrates below the canopy.

As I made my way upwards along another track, I noted that the hillside had been bared of almost all vegetation by rabbits. Only two species of plants, the Grass Trigger Plant and some bright yellow clustered everlastings, managed to survive and seemed virtually untouched by rabbits.

The open and unprotected nature of the surface of this very steep hill into which I had to dig my heels to take photographs safely, must encourage erosion and contribute to the instability of the cliffs along the Great Ocean

Road immediately below. The road is sometimes closed as a result of falling rock.

On the roadside cutting along the cliff face on the road immediately northeast of the Cumberland River is a well-known example of an ancient shore platform and a boulder bed. It was formed during the time of the last interglacial some 125,000 years ago. At that time the sea level must have been considerably higher than it is today because this relic shore platform is over seven metres above the present one. The sea retreated steadily during that period and at the peak of the last Ice Age, the shoreline must have been far out to sea. Eventually the ocean rose again as the glacial icecaps melted and the shoreline returned to its present position about 6,000 years ago.

It is possible to identify rounded sea-worn boulders in the cutting immediately above the old shore platform. The boulders on the face of the cutting exposed to the sea are much bigger than those exposed along the road as it turns inland to follow the course of the river. Thus the forces operating on this coastline must have been the same as those that apply today with the largest boulders being formed by the high-energy waves of the open sea.

I stayed on beyond nightfall at the Cumberland River to observe the insect life. Walking upriver in the dark with my gas lantern, I found a suitable group of rocks in the fast-running stream which supported both myself and the lantern safely. A mass of small black flies (family Simuliidae) were very soon attracted to the light and swarmed over the rocks on which it rested. Several species of this same family are painful biting flies, especially one kind which occurs in Queensland. But these particular individuals seemed singularly uninterested in my person. They were soon joined by much larger caddis flies. These latter insects are related to and superficially resemble moths. The larvae of caddis flies are associated with water and have quite elaborate cases in which they live and mature. They form a very important part in the diet of fish, notably trout.

There were also a few stoneflies about. Like caddis flies they are always associated with water, though unlike the latter their immature or nymphal stages are fully aquatic, living in the streams or along the margins of lakes. They are primitive insects well represented in southeast Australia, particularly in the Otways. Settled on the stone surfaces tonight, they were difficult to see by lantern light, their transparent wings and dull markings closely matching the colours of the rock.

Noctuid moth
(Cosmodes elegans).

213

ABOVE: A tiger moth
(Spilosoma glatignyi).

ABOVE RIGHT: Day-flying moth
(Epicoma contristis).

The next morning at Teddys Lookout, I photographed some striking bark patterns. They were the sort of colours you so often see in the autumn in the high country, perhaps not so colourful, yet subtle and striking in their own way.

Alongside the road I found a mauve flowered legume Twining Glycine, wound around a dead eucalypt twig. It is a very small, delicate and unobtrusive plant which could easily be overlooked, yet it is a first cousin of one of the world's most important crops and a major source of plant protein, the soy bean.

Unlike other broadacre crops, such as wheat and rice, or horticultural plants, such as the tomato, very limited use is being made of the wild stock in breeding programs. These other crops have benefited greatly by introduction of genes and naturally occurring cultivars, or closely related species, collected in their original environment. The Australian glycines – and Australia has the bulk of the species – are of particular interest because some exhibit resistance to Soy Bean Rust, a disease which in some seasons can destroy up to 30 per cent of the crop.

CSIRO is currently experimenting with other native glycines (Twining Glycine apparently does not hold much promise) to find ways by the traditional methods of plant breeding to introduce the resistant genes to soy bean. Progress is being made and already fertile hybrids have been produced. In the longer term, genetic engineering may offer greater possibility of success.

I made my way back to Melbourne by way of the Anglesea heathland and the Wormbete Road which forms a boundary between the heathy woodlands west of Anglesea township and the open farmland. I lunched at a spot on the heath where water has accumulated in the depressions and formed large puddles. These are now occupied by a variety of insects, most noticeably mosquito larvae which were everywhere very active. I noted how they rise quickly to the surface to absorb oxygen through the spiracles on the tips of their abdomens, then sink down again to the depths of the pond. The larvae, or wrigglers as they are often called, contrast strangely with the dark thickset and beetlelike pupae which are also very active. I was impressed with how mosquitoes are able to take advantage so quickly of a situation of abnormal late spring rainfall, occurring perhaps no more than once in 10 seasons, when puddles suddenly form and last only a few weeks.

A group of waterstriders caught my attention and proved infuriating subjects for photography, never remaining still for more than a second. The speed with which they can move over water is quite surprising. They are members of the order Hemiptera and hence related to plant bugs and harlequin bugs, but they are specifically adapted to life on the surface of water.

My last port of call today was the Bald Hills. The grass trees on the peak had attracted numerous ladybirds which were settled on the leaves. I have seen ladybirds behave in this way before, notably on mountain peaks in northeast Victoria where vast numbers may sometimes be found clustered together. It is believed they fly upwards to the most prominent local silhouette, a hill or a mountain, after an adequate feed on aphids. The theory is that the beetles accumulate in this manner to mate because the uncertain and erratic appearance of their principal food necessitates long periods of dormancy. After mating, the ladybirds disperse and are then able to exploit any rapid growth of aphid populations.

Ladybirds also prey on mealybugs, insects closely related to aphids. In fact, one of the great stories of biological control belongs to a species of Australian ladybird which overcame a succession of outbreaks of the Cottony Cushion Scale on citrus, at first in California and then later in several other countries. The scale, which is common in Southern Australia on a variety of native plants, causes little damage; when it found its way into California, however, it soon reached plague proportions, causing havoc in citrus groves. Fortunately, at about the same time, another outbreak in New Zealand was fortuitously brought under control by the chance introduction of another insect, a ladybird from Australia which was the scale's natural enemy. Specimens of this ladybird were collected near Adelaide, released in California, and quickly destroyed the Cottony Cushion Scale. Similar successes occurred in locations as widespread as India, where the scale had attacked tea plantations, and in Portugal, where it damaged citrus groves.

ABOVE: *A butterfly of the coastal wetlands, the Chrysotricha Skipper* (Hesperilla chrysotricha cyclospila).

BOTTOM LEFT: *Ladybird beetle* (Coccinella transversalis)

BOTTOM RIGHT: *Flower spider* (Diaea *sp*) *on everlasting* (Helichrysum *sp*).

11 DECEMBER

I left home at six o'clock this morning with a very doubtful forecast to cheer me up!

Today there were a number of plants in flower along the road between Gellibrand and the Otway Ridge. Fireweed is a prominent roadside plant in these parts and when in bloom, the brilliant masses of the small yellow daisy flowers add a welcome touch of colour to the uniform green of the forest. Dogwood with its flattened white flowering heads is beginning to become prominent too, particularly in the more open and partly cleared sites which suits its growth habit. On the road leading up to the Otway

Rushes line the banks of the Aire River.

Ridge, Christmas Bush is now making a great show with cascades of white and mauve tinted blossoms.

I reached my destination – the mouth of the Aire River – at 9.10 am. The weather was very dull and cloudy and seemingly unsuitable for photography. However, the extraordinarily still waters in the lower reaches of the Aire, which this year is landlocked by a sand bar, provided a millpond surface and some splendid reflections of old drowned fence lines, rushes and a wooden bridge which spans the river. This glasslike sheen, however, was soon disturbed by ripples as wind suddenly rose. Within minutes of my arrival the mirrorlike water had been replaced by a ruffled surface of myriad choppy waves.

A small flock of slow-flying Yellow-tailed Black Cockatoos, some 15 in number, made strange, low, clucking sounds as they flew over the bridge. Later I saw and photographed a pair swinging acrobatically on a small branch near the camping area. Although they eyed me curiously, they seemed unfazed by my efforts to photograph them – they have clearly become accustomed to the camp site and its regular visitors.

I walked down the western bank of the river after crossing the bridge taking a path through the narrow fringe of pasture which sprouted a surprising show of Strawberry Clover. The grassland extends for a couple of hundred metres and forms an apron at the base of the scrub-covered sand hills which rise to a height of 50 metres or so on the western side of the river just before its outlet into the ocean.

At one point on my walk a Little Black Cormorant emerged suddenly from the water and with much whirring and splashing flew excitedly away. How long can these birds remain submerged? To swim as effectively underwater as they do, they rely on their webbed feet which are something like those of a duck, although you are not aware of these when they are perched and certainly not when the cormorant is in flight.

At the bridge I saw Welcome Swallows wheeling about. It is surprising how often they choose man-made structures, such as a bridge, a hut or a verandah, as breeding sites. Other birds I noted included Crimson Rosellas, White-faced Herons and great numbers of thornbills, the latter as usual in small flocks feeding together.

This year the Aire River has not succeeded in reaching the ocean and a sand bar blocks its mouth. I assume it could be opened in two ways either from water flowing down the river and building up or alternatively from a storm where waves breach the sand bank and release the dammed-

ABOVE: *Yellow-Tailed Black Cockatoo, Aire River.*

BELOW: *Fruits of Prickly Tea Tree (Leptospermum juniperinum).*

up water. A chain of small lakes holds a considerable permanent body of water some kilometres back from the mouth.

A small group of sea birds occupied the rocks immediately to the west of the blocked entrance of the river. There were about 30 birds in all: Silver Gulls and Pacific Gulls, the latter much larger and resplendent in black and white plumage. With the huge seas pounding in behind the birds it was a scene made for a long-focal-length photograph.

The jumbled mass of jagged limestone rocks west of the mouth of the Aire is an extraordinary sight. It forms a very rough platform which took me a considerable time to negotiate because of the very sharp and tumbled rocks. The Aire River formation is part of the extensive dune limestone cliffs which run westward towards Glenaire and enclose the flood plain of the Aire River. The profile of the cliffs above the shore platform displays some striking rock formations. In some places narrow beds of limestone a few centimetres in width have been laid down on top of one another and at a distance look like so many razor blades, the rows of blades or shelves often aligned at crazy angles to each other as though some giant earthquake broke up the original strata and redistributed it.

On the heathland near Port Campbell, I found and photographed a pink Paper Flower which sports twin flowers on a terminal head, both the leaves and flowers being very furry. I also filmed the strikingly marked and coloured fruits of tea tree. The fruits are green in colour but the openings of the seed chamber are boldly marked as red crosses.

15 & 16 DECEMBER

My plan today was to catch the sunrise at Point Roadknight and then on to Point Franklin, Lavers Hill, Moonlight Beach and home tomorrow morning.

It was too high a tide and too calm a sea to provide the sort of early morning sunrise I had hoped for. Also it was a little too late. It is the

Sunrise through a jellyfish (unidentified), or close encounters of a third kind!

218

very first moments of sunrise that produce the most beautiful effects and which momentarily transform a breaking wave into an opalescent mass of colour. Instead I had to content myself with the photography of some reflections from the wash of the waves and the silhouetted outline of jagged calcarenite pinnacles at the easterly end of this very slender and fragile peninsula. A number of sponges had washed in making a line of flotsam together with numerous small shells and seaweeds. In one instance I photographed three quite distinct sponges lying side by side and if, as it appears to my untutored eye, they were different species, it gives some idea of the richness of variety among this little-studied group of primitive sea animals. These were, of course, only the skeletons of the original living sponges which are found at depth off the shore and are usually washed in as a result of storms.

The seaweeds were mainly of one species, delicate fernlike and white

ABOVE: Hanging moss (Weymouthia sp), Maites Rest.

BELOW: A coat-of-mail shell chiton (Poneroplax albida).

BOTTOM RIGHT: Shells in rock pool, Point Franklin. Beaked mussels (Brachydontes rostratus), limpets (Patelloida latistrigata) and false limpets (Siphonaria diemenensis).

OPPOSITE PAGE: Johanna Beach, looking east from near Deep Creek.

in colour. I doubt whether this is the natural colour of the species; it was probably one of the red seaweeds that bleach on exposure to sunlight and air. These particular seaweeds, like sponges, are usually associated with deeper water.

On the way to Point Franklin I detoured to take in the beautiful gully at Maites Rest which I knew well from visits years ago. Now much overgrown, the track to it can still be followed through, although in places fallen trees block the path. In one spot I passed a huge ancient Myrtle Beech. Over the hundreds of years that it has stood here much of the soil along the creek has eroded away, exposing a great, gnarled root system. The original soil surface must have been three metres above the present level. The track enables you to walk easily through and under the original roots which now appear as multiple trunks of a single tree. It gives some idea of the huge soil losses that occur over time.

Later at Point Franklin I cautiously approached two Little Black Cormorants that were perched on a rock above a large pool exposed at low tide. They were too wary to allow me to photograph them closely and quickly flew off. I noted that the pool was well stocked with whitebait about 12 to 15 centimetres long and these small fish may well have been the subject of the cormorants' interest. Nearby, a Pied Oystercatcher was less shy and I did manage to photograph it before it, too, flew away. I was disappointed that there was no sign today of the plovers I had seen previously on this lonely stretch of sandy beach.

The large expanses of shore platform exposed this morning at Point Franklin proved ideal for the observation of rock pools. There were many species of seaweeds, molluscs, starfish, chitons and small fish, all perfectly visible in the crystal clear water of the pools. Some chitons I saw occupied the top surface of the seaward edge of the rock platform and were continually washed by incoming waves. These unusual shells looked to be armour plated and are sometimes called coat of mail shells. They were liberally covered with marine growth which hid their strange yet very symmetrical outline. Chitons are ancient molluscs represented in fossil beds millions of years old and are strangely sensitive to light, especially those which live beneath stones and rocks during the daylight. They will quickly move towards the shade if exposed to sunlight. Chitons have eyes located in pores in the shell plates which in turn are connected to nerve endings in the skin. It has been estimated that as many as 8,500 eyes may be present on the surface of a single specimen. You often see the individual plates of chiton shells

washed up with other shells on the beach, frequently they are blue in colour and because of their shape are sometimes called butterfly shells.

Among a rock pool of limpets that I photographed were some small but boldly striped black and white individuals. These were false limpets belonging to the family Siphonariidae. Surprisingly they are more closely related to the common garden snail and to slugs than to the true limpets alongside them in the pool. The pulmonates to which garden snails and false limpets (Siphonaria) belong are mostly air breathers and, in adapting to a marine environment, the false limpets have developed a gill-like organ in place of what was originally a lung (mantle cavity). Because they have shared a similar environment with the true limpets, they have evolved a similar shell shape.

After lunch I drove to Johanna Beach. I had hoped to walk westward from there to Lion Head but the high tide, the stinging sand and salt spray made this all but impossible. Instead I made my way along the clifftop where pastures had been sown right to the edge many years ago and are still grazed.

In places the pasture was dominated by Yorkshire Fog, a soft, downy-leaved grass, native to the northern hemisphere and first recorded as naturalised in Victoria in 1878. Usually classed as an inferior species and often an indicator of potash deficiency, fog nevertheless can and does support high milk production in some well-watered dairying regions.

From the high seaward cliffs the pastures fall steeply away to the northeast and form part of the valley of the Blue Johanna River. Here it is an extaordinarily serpentine stream and, viewed from high above, the deep incised meanders on the grassy flats look as though at any moment they could wriggle to life.

At one point high above the beach I took shelter from the howling wind behind some low scrub and looked back eastward towards Cape Otway. It was a striking, stormy scene. Immediately below the pasture the cliff had fallen away to reveal soil extraordinarily rich in shades of purple and dark red, and which supported a few precariously perched plants of tussock grass.

The cliffs along this stretch of coastline are cut by two streams, Deep Creek and Knowledge Creek. The first is distinguished by an array of grotesquely shaped rocks on the beach immediately east of the entrance. I clambered over these finding concretions in the shapes of anvils, dumbbells, spheres and eggs, and sections pitted with square metres of honeycomb weathering and other surfaces eroded into what looked like miniature sand dunes.

Knowledge Creek is less spectacular and is characterised by a hanging valley, the stream dropping directly from a ledge several metres to the beach below, and by two small caves. The name of this creek has always intrigued me. It was given by La Trobe when he covered this coastal route

Summer evening after thunderstorm, Lavers Hill.

Cultivation patterns near Lavers Hill.

on his third and successful trip to Cape Otway in April 1846. He named it after an unfortunate carpenter, a Mr Knowledge, who had earlier accompanied Captain Irvine, the skipper of the ill-fated *Johanna*, and Mr William Allen, a grazier of the Hopkins River near Warrnambool, on a reconnaissance trip to establish whether the *Johanna* could be refloated. In his account of his journey, La Trobe claimed that it was at this creek, presumably an overnight camp, that Knowledge met with an unfortunate accident. Knowledge apparently accidentally ignited his power flask, blowing some fingers off. Local history has it that in the cold, blustery conditions, he was warming his hands and his backside rather too close to the fire when a spark set the flask off!

Irvine eventually decided that the *Johanna* was unsalvageable and returned with his companions to Allen's Station. A later boat journey by a crew of four to investigate the wreck was a disaster and two crew members were drowned. The survivors made it back to the station and later one of the survivors alerted unruly elements in the town of Portland to the nature of the ship's cargo: sugar, flour and particularly cherry brandy. As La Trobe described it, a willing party was recruited for 'Xmas jollification'. The result was a six-week binge 'every man but one becoming blind by exposure and fly bites'. The debauched and exhausted party finally found their way to Allen's Station on the Hopkins River 'led by the seeing man with a stick'!

The small hamlet of Lavers Hill was much less windy than Johanna Beach had been and several local farmers were busily engaged in the cultivation of potato fields. It was an attractive scene with newly ploughed red-brown soil and lush green pastures. The graceful contours of this country highlighted the deep plough lines which formed whirling patterns in one field and served to emphasise the smooth and rounded undulations of the landscape of the Otway Ridge.

It was low tide at Moonlight Beach that evening and as I wandered along the narrow fringe of moist sand at the edge of a large rock pool, I reflected on the passing of the year. Summer is with us once again and with it have come the changes this season brings – the honeyed scent of the flowering Messmates and Brown Stringybarks and the piercing song of cicadas in the woodlands, the cascading white blossoms of Christmas Bushes in the gullies and the persistent irritation of march flies on the beaches. And yet, the world of nature is so varied and so unpredictable that when I return to this unique and beautiful area next year and in the years that follow, I know I will always discover something new and fascinating. It was with this heartening thought that I turned and headed for home.

BIBLIOGRAPHY

Abele C, 'Explanatory Notes on Anglesea 1:63,360 Geological Map', Geological Survey of Victoria report, 1968.

Abele C, *Geology of the Anglesea Area, Central Coastal Victoria*, Geological Survey of Victoria, memoir 31, 1979.

Abercrombie M, Hickman CJ & Johnson ML, *The Penguin Dictionary of Biology*, 7th edn, Penguin, England, 1986.

Andersen Alan, 'The Ants of Southern Australia', *A Guide to the Bassian Fauna*, CSIRO, Australia, 1991.

Angair, White Mary (ed), *Anglesea, A Natural History Study by Angair*, 7th edn, 1987.

Armstrong JA, 'Biotic pollination mechanisms in the Australian flora–a review', *New Zealand Journal of Botany*, vol 17, 1979, pp 467–508.

Arnold Don & Shackleton Alec, *Colac Region Proposed Coastal Management Plan*, Colac Region Department of Conservation and Environment, Victoria, March, 1991.

Ashton DH, 'Studies of Flowering Behaviour in *Eucalyptus regnans* F Muell', *Australian Journal of Botany*, 23, 1975, pp 399–411.

Ashton DH, 'Studies of Litter in *Eucalyptus regnans* Forests', *Australian Journal of Botany*, 23, 1975, pp 413–33.

Ashton DH, 'Tall Open-forests in Australian Vegetation' in *Australian Vegetation*, Groves RH (ed), Cambridge University Press, 1981, pp 121–151.

Ashton DH, 'The Development of Even-aged Stands of *Eucalyptus regnans* F Muell in Central Victoria', *Australian Journal of Botany*, 24, 1976, pp 397–414.

Audas JW & Daley BA, 'The Great Ocean Road', *Victorian Naturalist*, vol L, 1933, pp 95–106.

Australian Parliament, *Fifth Progress Report of the Royal Commission on State Forests and Timber Reserves. The Otway Forest: Its Resources, Management, and Control*, Parl Papers 1899–1900, vol 4, pp 451–466.

Baker G, 'Geology and Physiography of the Moonlight Head District, Victoria', *Proceedings of the Royal Society of Victoria*, vol 60, 1950, pp 17–44.

Baker G, 'Heavy Black Sands on Some Victorian Beaches', *Journal of Sedimentary Petrology*, vol 15, no 1, 1945, pp 11–19.

Baker George, 'Tektites from the Sherbrook River District, East of Port Campbell', *Proceedings of the Royal Society of Victoria*, vol 49, pt II, 1937, p 165.

Baker HG & Baker I, 'Some Anthecological Aspects of the Evolution of Nectar Producing Flowers, Particularly Amino Acid Production in Nectar' in *Taxonomy and Ecology*, VH Heywood (ed), Academic Press, London and New York, 1973.

Balmford R, 'Early Introductions of Birds of Victoria', *The Australian Bird Watcher*, vol 7 (7), 1978.

Bardwell Sandra, 'The Otways: Wonderful Coastal Walking Within Reach of Melbourne', *Australian Wild*, vol 4 (2), 1984, pp 66–68.

Barrett C, 'Stray Notes on Stone-flies', *Victorian Naturalist*, vol XLIII, 1927, p 260.

Barson MM & Calder DM, 'The Vegetation of the Victorian Coast', *Proceedings of the Royal Society of Victoria*, 92 (1), pp 55–65.

Bartlett AG, 'Multiple-use Hardwood Forest Management in the Otway Ranges', *Australian Forestry*, 46 (4), 1983, pp 278–286.

Beasley AW, 'Heavy Black Sands From Phillip Island', vol 21, National Museum of Victoria, Melbourne, pp 101–115.

Bird ECF, *Sites of Special Scientific Interest in the Victorian Coastal Region. A Report on Geological and Geomorphological Aspects*, Town and Country Planning Board, Melbourne, 1977.

Blackmore John AP, 'An Australian Orchid Emigrant', *Victorian Naturalist*, June, 1960, pp 46–47.

Bonwick J, Sayers CE (ed), *Western Victoria: Its Geography, Geology and Social Condition. The Narrative of an Educational Tour in 1867*, Griffin Press, Adelaide, 1970.

Brown AHD, Grant JE, Burdon JJ, Grace JP & Pullen R, 'Collection and Utilization of Wild Perennial Glycine', World Soybean Research Conference III, Richard Shibles (ed), Westview Press Inc, Boulder and London, 1985.

Brown PL, *Narrative of George Russell*, Oxford University Press, Melbourne, 1935.

Bureau of Flora and Fauna, *Flora of Australia*, Australian Government Publishing Service, Canberra, vol 1, 1981.

Busby JR & Bridgewater PB, 'Studies in Victorian Vegetation, 11A, Floristic Survey of Vegetation Associated with *Nothofagus Cunninghamii* (Hook) Oerst in Victoria and Tasmania', *Proceedings of the Royal Society of Victoria*, 89, pp 173–182.

Cadwalladcr PL & Backhouse GN, *A Guide to the Freshwater Fish of Victoria*, Victorian Government Printing Office, Melbourne, 1983.

Caire NJ, 'Notes on the Giant Trees of Victoria', *Victorian Naturalist*, November, 1904.

Calder DM, 'Nature in National Parks', *Parkwatch*, 127, 1981.

Cantrill DJ & Douglas JG, 'Mycorrhizal Conifer Roots from the Lower Cretaceous of the Otway Basin, Victoria', *Australian Journal of Botany*, vol 36, 1988, pp 257–272.

Carr GW, 'Vegetation of the Cape Otway Parker Area', Supplement to *Geelong Naturalist*, vol 8, no 1, 1971.

Carroll Elizabeth J & Ashton DH, 'Seed Storage in Soils of Several Victorian Plant Communities', *Victorian Naturalist*, vol 82, 1965, pp 102–103.

Christophel David C, 'Occurrence of Casuarina Mega Fossils in the Tertiary of South East Australia', *Journal of Botany*, vol 28, pp 249–259.

Clark ID, *Aboriginal Languages and Clans: An Historical Atlas of Western and Central Victoria, 1800–1900*, Monash Publications in Geography, no 37, Monash University, Victoria, 1990.

Cochrane GR, 'Ecological Valence of Mountain Ash (*Eucalyptus regnans* F Muell) as a key to its distribution', *Victorian Naturalist*, vol 86, 1969, pp 6–10.

Coleman E, 'Further Notes on the Pollination of *Cryptostylis subulata* (Labill) Reichb', *Victorian Naturalist*, vol L, 1933, pp 41–44.

Coleman E, 'Pollination of *Cryptostylis subulata* (Labill) Reichb', *Victorian Naturalist*, vol XLVI, 1929, pp 62–66.

Coleman E, 'Pollination of the Orchid *Crypostylis leptochila*', *Victorian Naturalist*, vol XLIV, 1927, pp 20–22.

Common IFB, *Moths of Australia*, Melbourne University Press, Melbourne, 1990.

Common IFB & Waterhouse DF, *Butterflies of Australia*, Angus & Robertson, Sydney, 1981.

Coppinger RP, 'The effect of experience and novelty on avian feeding behaviour with reference to the evolution of warning coloration in butterflies II Reactions of native birds to novel insects', *The American Naturalist*, vol 104, no 938, 1970.

Corris P, *Aborigines and Europeans in Western Victoria*, AIAS, Canberra, 1968.

Costermans Leon, *Native Trees and Shrubs of South Eastern Australia*, Rigby, 1983.

Coutts PJF, 'Coastal Archaeology in Victoria Part 1', *Proceedings of the Royal Society of Victoria*, 1981, vol 92, pp 62–80.

Cowley RD, *Notes on the Otway Ranges*, Forest Commission, Victoria, 1971.

Cox JB, 'Short-tailed Shearwater Colonies of the South-East', *South Australian Ornithologist*, vol 28, 1978, p 16.

Crook Keith, 'The break-up of the Australian-Antarctic segment of Gondwanaland', *Ecological Biogeography of Australia*, vol 1.

CSIRO, *The Insects Of Australia*, 2nd edn, vol I & II, Melbourne University Press, 1991.

Da Costa Grant, 'Otway forest giants', *Park Watch*, vol 4, 137, 1984, pp 28–29.

Dafni A & Calder DM, 'Pollination by deceit and floral mimesis in *Thelymitra antennifera* (Orchidaceae)', *Plant Systematics and Evolution*, 158, Springer-Verlag, 1987, pp 11–22.

Dakins WJ, *Australian Seashores*, fully revised and illustrated by Isobel Bennett, Angus & Robertson, Sydney, 1987.

Daley C, 'Food of Australian Aborigines', *Victorian Naturalist*, XLVIII, 1930, pp 23–31.

Dettman Mary E, 'The Cretaceous Flora', *Ecological Biogeography of Australia*, 11, pp 355–376.

Douglas JG, 'Aborigines in the Ranges', *Victorian Naturalist*, vol 95, 1978, pp 222–225.

Douglas JG, 'The Geology of the Otway Region, Southern Victoria', *Proceedings of the Royal Society of Victoria*, vol 89, pts I & II, pp 19–25.

Douglas JG, 'The Mesozoic Floras of Victoria, Part 3', *Geological Survey of Victoria*, memoir 29, 1973.

Douglas JG & Ferguson JA (eds), *Geology of Victoria*, Department of Industry, Technology and Resources, Government of Victoria, Melbourne, 1988.

Douglas JG & Laing ACM, '1976/4 Explanatory Notes on the Colac 1:250,000 Geological Map', Geological Survey of Victoria report, Mines Department of Victoria, Melbourne.

Dring MJ, 'Germination and Attachment of Spores', *The Biology of Marine Plants*, Edward Arnold, 1982.

Duncan Betty & Isaac Golda, *Ferns and Allied Plants of Victoria, Tasmania, and South Australia*, Melbourne University Press in association with Monash University, Melbourne, 1986.

Earl GE & Bennett AP, *A Survey of the flora and fauna in four catchments of the Gellibrand River Basin, Otway Ranges, Victoria*, Rural Water Commission, Victoria, by the Department of Conservation, Forests and Lands, Victoria, Arthur Rylah Institute for Environmental Research.

Edwards AB, 'Notes of the geology of the Lorne District, Victoria', *Proceedings of the Royal Society of Victoria*, vol 75, 1962, pp 101–119.

Edwards AB & Baker G, 'Jurassic Arkose in Southern Victoria', *Proceedings of the Royal Society of Victoria*, vol 55, pt II, 1943.

Ellis Clarence, *The Pebbles On The Beach*, Faber & Faber, London.

Ewart AJ, *Flora of Victoria*, Victorian Government, 1930.

Farrell PW & Novotny PM, 'Hardwood Harvesting and Water Quality in the Otways, 2 West Barwon Catchment', Conservation, Forests and Lands Research report, no 321.

Filson Rex B & Rogers Roderick, *Lichens of South Australia*, Government of South Australia, 1979.

Ford H, 'The Value of Insects and Nectar to Honeyeaters', *The Emu*, 1976, p 83.

Forests Commission of Victoria, *A Brief Description of the Forest Types, Geology and Other Features of the Otway District*, Melbourne, 1934.

Fox Paul, 'Over the Garden Fence', *Historic Environment*, vol IV (3), 1985, pp 29–36.

Fripp Yvonne J, 'Mating System and Cross-compatibility of Races of *Epacris impressa*', *Australian Journal of Botany*, vol 30, 1982, pp 131–8.

Frith HJ (ed), *Birds in the Australian High Country*, revised edn, Angus & Robertson, Sydney, 1984.

Fuhrer Bruce, *A Field Companion to Australian Fungi*, Five Mile Press, Hawthorn, 1985.

Gabriel Joseph, 'Further Notes On the Mutton Birds of Bass Strait', *Victorian Naturalist*, vol XXVIII, 1912, pp 206–207.

Galbraith Jean, *Collins Field Guide to the Wild Flowers of South-East Australia*, William Collins, London, 1977.

Garnett J Ros, 'Out Jungle-Weed!', *Victorian Naturalist*, vol 82, 1965, p 225.

Gell Robert A, 'Shelly Beaches on the Victorian Coast', *Proceedings of the Royal Society of Victoria*, 90 (142), 1978, pp 257–269.

Gill AM, 'Post-Settlement Fire History in Victorian Landscapes', *Fire in the Australian Biota*, Gill AM, Groves RH & Noble IR (eds), Australian Academy of Science, Canberra, 1981, pp 77–95.

Gill ED, 'Aboriginal Kitchen Middens and Marine Shell Bed', *Mankind*, 4, University of Sydney, pp 249–254.

Gill ED, 'Large Waves at Lorne, Victoria', *Victorian Naturalist*, vol 93, 1976, p 92.

Gill ED, 'Channels in Shore Platforms–a World of their Own', *Victorian Naturalist*, vol 93, 1976, pp 216–220.

Gill ED, 'Prehistoric Wildfires in SE Australia', *Victorian Naturalist*, vol 90, 1973, pp 347–348.

Gill, ED, 'Some Effects of Drought, Bushfire and Floods on the Otway Coast of Victoria', *Victorian Naturalist*, vol 101, no 2, 1984, pp 92–94.

Gill ED & McNeill Nancy, 'The Otway Coast of Victoria, Australia', *Victorian Naturalist*, vol 90, 1973, pp 12–14.

Gill ED, Segnit ER & McNeill NH, 'Concretions in Otway Group Sediments, South-East Australia', *Proceedings of the Royal Society of Victoria*, 89, pp 51–55.

Grant Andrew, *The Vegetation of Port Campbell National Park*, Department of Conservation, Forests and Lands, 1987.

Greenslade PJM, 'A Guide to Ants of South Australia', Special Educational Bulletin Series, South Australia Museum, Adelaide, 1979.

Hall TS & Pritchard CB, 'The Tertiary Deposits of the Aire and Cape Otway', *Proceedings of the Royal Society of Victoria*, 1899, vol XII, pp 35–68.

Hall TS, 'Art XI–Notes on the Geology of the County about Anglesea', *Proceedings of the Royal Society of Victoria*, vol 23, pt I, 1910, pp 44–45.

Hardy AD, 'Australia's Great Trees', *Victorian Naturalist*, vol LI, 1935, pp 231–241.

Hardy AD, 'The Measuring of Tall Trees', *Victorian Naturalist*, vol XXXIX, 1923, pp 166–167.

Hardy AD, 'The Tall Trees Of Australia', *Victorian Naturalist*, vol XXXV, 1918, pp 46–55.

Harris SG, *A Preliminary Study of Plant Succession on Harvested Sites in the Otway Ranges: Wye Road Regeneration Area, Research Report 316*, Public Land Management and Forests Division, 1986.

Hewitt JM, 'Cattle Egret in Australia', *The Emu*, vol 69, 1969.

Heyligers Petrus C, 'The Impact of Introduced Plants on Foredune Formation in South-eastern Australia', *Proceedings of the Ecological Society of Australia*, 14, pp 23–41.

Hills Sherbon, 'Shore Platforms and Wave Ramps', *Geological Magazine*, vol 109, no 2, 1972, pp 81–192.

Hinton HE, '*Myrmecophilous Lycaenidae* and other Lepidoptera–a Summary', *Proceedings and Transactions*, South London Entomological and Natural History Society, 1949–50, pp 111–175.

Houghton Norm, *Sawdust and Steam: A History of the Railway and Tramways of the Eastern Otway Ranges*, Light Railway Research Society of Australia, Melbourne, 1975.

Houghton Norm, *West Otways Narrow Gauge*, Light Railway Research Society of Australia, no 45, vol XII, 1973, pp 1–51.

Howard TM, 'Southern Closed Forests', *Australian Vegetation*, Cambridge University Press, 1981, pp 102–120.

Howard Truda & Ashton DH, 'The Distribution of *Nothofagus cunninghamii* Rainforest', *Proceedings of the Royal Society of Victoria*, 86, pp 47–76.

Hughes Gary, 'On The Right Track', *The Australian Magazine*, August, 1992.

Hyam GN, 'The Vegetable Foods of the Australian Aboriginals', *Victorian Naturalist*, vol LVI, 1939, pp 95–98.

Ingold CT, *The Biology of Fungi*, 4th edn, Hutchinson, London, 1981.

Jenkin JJ, 'Evolution of the Victorian Coastline', *Proceedings of the Royal Society of Victoria*, 1981, 92 (1), pp 37–55.

Jones David, *Native Orchids of Australia*, Reed Books, Australia, 1988.

Jones DL & Clemesha SC, *Australian Ferns and Fern Allies*, 2nd edn, AH & AW Reed, Sydney, 1982.

Jutson JT, 'Notes on the Coastal Physiography of Port Campbell, Victoria', *Proceedings of the Royal Society of Victoria*, 40, pt 1, 1927.

Jutson JT, 'The Shore Platforms of Lorne, Victoria, and the Processes of Erosion Operating Thereon', *Proceedings of the Royal Society of Victoria*, vol 65.

Kershaw AP, 'Quaternary vegetation and environments', *Ecological Biogeography of Australia*, 5, pp 81–102.

Kiddle Margaret, *Men Of Yesterday. A Social History of the Western District of Victoria 1834–1890*, Melbourne University Press, Melbourne, 1961.

Koenig WL, *The History of the Winchelsea Shire*, Winchelsea Shire Council, Colac, 1933.

Ladiges Pauline & Ashton DH, 'A comparison of some populations of *Eucalyptus viminalis* Labill, growing on calcareous and acid soils in Victoria, Australia', *Australian Journal of Ecology*, vol 2, 1977, pp 161–178.

Land Conservation Council of Victoria, 'Report on the Corangamite Study Area', Melbourne, 1976.

Laseron Charles, *Ancient Australia*, 3rd edn, revised by Rudolf Oskar Brunschweiler, Angus & Robertson, Sydney, 1984.

La Trobe CJ, 'Memoranda of Journals, Excursions and Absences 1839–1854', ms no H93166, State Library of Victoria.

Linforth DJ, 'The Climate of the Otway Region', *Proceedings of the Royal Society of Victoria*, vol 89, pp 61–68.

Lloyd FE, 'Further notes on Australian *Utricularia* with a correction', *Victorian Naturalist*, vol LIII, 1937, p 163.

Lobban CS, Harrison PS & Duncan MJ, *The Physiological Ecology of Seaweeds*, Cambridge University Press, 1985.

Loney JK, *Otway Memories*, Maritime History Publications, Geelong, 1971.

Loney JK, *Wrecks Along The Great Ocean Road*, published by author, 8th edn, 1967.

Lourandos Harry, 'Aboriginal Settlement and Land Use in South Western Victoria: A Report on Current Field Work', *The Artefact*, vol 1 (4), 1976, pp 174–193.

MacPherson J Hope & Gabriel CJ, *Marine Molluscs Of Victoria*, Melbourne University Press in association with the National Museum of Victoria, 1962.

Main Barbara, *Spiders*, 2nd edn, William Collins, Sydney, 1984.

Malicky H, 'New Aspects of the Association between Lycaenid Larvae (Lycaenidae) and Ants (Formicidae, Hymenoptera)', *Journal of the Lepidopterists Society*, vol 24, no 3, 1970, pp 190–202.

Marine Research Group of Victoria, *Coastal Invertebrates of Victoria: An Atlas of Selected Species*, Marine Research Group of Victoria in association with the Museum of Victoria, Melbourne, 1984.

Marks GC, Fuhrer BA & Walters NEM, *Tree Diseases in Victoria*, Forest Commission, Victoria.

Martin Helene, 'The Tertiary Flora', *Ecological Biogeography of Australia*, 13, pp 393–406.

Mascord Ramon, *Australian Spiders in Colour*, AH & AW Reed, Wellington, 1970.

Massola A, 'The Grinding Rocks at Gellibrand', *Victorian Naturalist*, vol 79, 1962, pp 66–67.

Meredith Dr Charles, *The Vegetation of the Anglesea Lease Area*, Land Conservation Council, Melbourne, 14 November, 1986.

Monastersky Richard, 'Dinosaurs In The Dark', *Science News*, vol 133, p 184.

Morgan John, *The Life and Adventures of William Buckley*, first published by Macdougall, Hobart, 1852; this edn Heinemann, London, 1967, pp 1–29.

Morrison GE, Rosamund Duruz (ed), *The Long Walk*, PAP Book Company, Victoria, 1979.

Morrow PA, Bellas TE & Eisner T, 'Eucalyptus Oils in the Defensive Oral Discharge of Australian Sawfly Larvae (Hymenoptera: Pergidae)', *Oecologia*, 24, Berlin, 1976, pp 193–206.

Mulvaney DJ, 'Archaeological Excavations on the Aire River, Otway Peninsula, Victoria', *Proceedings of the Royal Society of Victoria*, vol 77 (2), 1960, pp 1–15.

Nicholls WH, *Orchids of Australia*, Thomas Nelson, 1969.

O'Keefe JA, 'The Tektite Problem', *Scientific American*, September, 1979.

Parsons RF, Kirkpatrick JB & Carr GW, 'Native Vegetation of the Otway Region, Victoria', *Proceedings of the Royal Society of Victoria*, vol 89, 1977, pp 77–88.

Parsons WT, *Noxious Weeds of Victoria*, Inkata Press, Australia, 1973.

Patton Reuben, 'The Factors Controlling the Distribution of Trees in Victoria', *Proceedings of the Royal Society of Victoria*, vol 42, pt 11, 1930.

Pearl Cyril, *Morrison of Peking*, Angus & Robertson, Sydney, 1967.

Pescott Trevor, *The Otways*, Rigby, 1976.

Pitt AJ, *A Study of the Land in the Catchments of the Otway Range and Adjacent Plains*, Soil Conservation Authority, Victoria.

Port Fairy Borough Council, 'Marram Grass–A Wonderful Sand Stay', *News Print*, Port Fairy.

Presland Gary, *An Archaeological Survey of the Otway Forest Region*, report to the Environmental Studies Division, (ess no 382).

Pryor LD & Johnson LAS, 'Eucalyptus, the Universal Australian', *Ecological Biogeography of Australia*, 17, 1982, pp 499–536.

Raff Janet, 'Hatching Process of Cicada', *Victorian Naturalist*, vol XLIII, 1927, pp 200–204.

Raggatt HG & Crespin I, 'Stratigraphy of Tertiary Rocks between Torquay and Eastern View, Victoria', *Proceedings of the Royal Society of Victoria*, 67, pp 75–142.

Rainforest Technical Committee, *Rainforest Conservation In Victoria*, a Report to the Minister for Conservation, Forests and Lands and the Minister for Planning and Environment, February, 1986.

Ramsbottom John, *Mushrooms and Toadstools*, Collins, London, 1953.

Recher Harry F, 'Nectar-feeding and its evolution among Australian vertebrates', *Ecological Biogeography of Australia*, p 1639.

Rich Thomas & Rich Patricia, 'Polar Dinosaurs and Biotas of the Early Cretaceous of South Eastern Australia', *National Geographic Research*, 5 (1), 1989, pp 15–53.

Richards Thomas, 'A predictive model of archaeological site distribution and density in the Otway Range, Victoria', February, 1992.

Rogers RW & Stevens GN, 'Lichens', *Ecological Biogeography of Australia*, p 593.

Rosengren Neville, *Sites of Geological and Geomorphological Significance in the Shire of Otway*, Ministry of Conservation, Victoria, 1984.

Scarlett NH, 'The Aborigines of the Otway Region', *Proceedings of the Royal Society of Victoria*, 1977, vol 89.

Schwartz Larry, 'The Long and Winding Road', *Sunday Age*, 31 May, 1992.

Serventy DL, *Mutton-birding Bass Strait, Australia's Last Frontier*, Australian Broadcasting Commission, 1969, pp 53–60.

Simpson Ken & Day Nicholas, *The Birds of Australia*, Lloyd O'Neill, 1984.

Slack Adrian, photographs by Jane Gate, *Carnivorous Plants*, AH & AW Reed.

Sloane H, 'Reminiscences of Hugh Hamilton Gibson: A Pioneer', *Victorian Historical Society Magazine*, October, 1956.

Smart Paul, *The Illustrated Encyclopedia of the Butterfly World in Colour*, Corgi, London, 1981.

Smith Brian, 'Victorian Non-marine Molluscs', *Victorian Naturalist*, vol 87, 1970, pp 248–249.

Smith Roger, 'Time to Conserve the Otways after a Century of Ruin', *Habitat*, 1983, pp 2–5.

Specht RL, 'Evolution Of The Australian Flora: Some Generalisations', *Ecological Biogeography of Australia*, 27, pp 783–806.

Specht RL, 'Responses to Fires in Heathlands and Related Shrublands' in *Fire and the Australian Biota*, Gill AM, Groves RH & Noble IR (eds), Australian Academy of Science, Canberra, 1981, pp 394–415.

Stace Helen & Fripp Yvonne, 'Raciation of *Epacris impressa*. I Corolla Colour and Corolla Length', *Australian Journal of Botany*, 1977, vol 25, pp 299–314.

Stace Helen & Fripp Yvonne, 'Raciation of *Epacris impressa*. II Habitat Differences and Flowering Times', *Australian Journal of Botany*, 1977, vol 25, pp 315–23.

Stace Helen & Fripp Yvonne, 'Raciation of *Epacris impressa*. III Polymorphic Populations', *Australian Journal of Botany*, 1977, vol 25, pp 325–36.

Strahan Ronald (ed), *Complete Book of Australian Mammals*, Angus & Robertson, Sydney, 1983.

Stuart IMF, 'Ethno-history in the Otway Ranges', *The Artefact*, 6, pp 79–88.

Taylor Jan, *Flower Power in the Australian Bush and Garden: The Fascinating Inter-relationship Between Insects and Plants*, Kangaroo Press, 1989.

Tillyard RJ, *The Insects Of Australia And New Zealand*, Angus & Robertson, Sydney, 1924.

Tindale NB, 'Revision of the Australian Ghost Moths (*Lepidoptera homoneura*, Family

Hepialidae)', Records of the South Australian Museum, vol V, no 3, 1935, pp 275–332.

Trotter Kenneth, 'Australites (Tektites), The How, Why, and Where', *Victorian Naturalist*, vol 85, 1968, pp 344–347.

Turner JS, Carr Stella & Bird ECF, 'The dune succession at Corner Inlet, Victoria', *Proceedings of the Royal Society of Victoria*, vol 75, pp 17–33.

[Unknown], 'A Victorian Jarosite Deposit', *Chemical Engineering and Mining Review*, March 5, 1921, p 199.

[Unknown], 'Disastrous Wreck off Cape Otway. The *Eric The Red* with American Exhibits. Total loss of the vessel', *Age*, September 6, 1880.

[Unknown], 'Jarosite: A Source of Potash', *Chemical Engineering and Mining Review*, April 5, 1921.

[Unknown], 'The Loss of the *Marie Gabrielle* Off Moonlight Head', *Argus*, 30 November, 1869.

[Unknown], Wreck of the Barque *Fiji, Argus*, September 7, 1891.

[Unknown], Wreck of the Barque *Fiji, Leader*, September 12, 1891.

Wagstaff BE & Mason JMc, 'Palynological Dating of Lower Cretaceous Coastal Vertebrate Localities, Victoria, Australia', *National Geographic Research*, 5 (1), 1989, pp 54–63.

Walker Donald, Beacons of Hope: *An Early History of Cape Otway and King Island Lighthouses*, Neptune, 1981.

Wark Margaret, White Mary, Robertson David & Marriott Philip, 'Regeneration of Heath and Heath Woodland in the North-eastern Otway Ranges Following the Wildfire of February 1983', *Proceedings of the Royal Society of Victoria*, vol 99, no 2, 1987, pp 51–88.

Watson Jeanette, 'Diver's Diary', *Victorian Naturalist*, vol 83, 1966, pp 174–175.

Weste Gretna, 'The Truth About Cinnamon Fungus', *Victorian National Parks Association Journal*, vol 109, 1977.

Wheeler Jack, 'South African Bone-Seed Becoming A Curse', *Victorian Naturalist*, vol 87, 1964, pp 225–226.

White Mary, *The Flowers of Anglesea River Valley*, Lutheran Publishing House, Adelaide, 1989.

Whitten DGA with Brooks JRV, *The Penguin Dictionary of Geology*, Penguin, Ringwood, 1986.

Williams LB, 'Otways–Coastal Forest' *Victorian National Parks Association*, no 108, 1977, pp 20–22.

Williams LB, 'Timber Production In The Otway Region', *Proceedings of Royal Society of Victoria*, vol 89, pts I & II, pp 89–97.

Willis JH, 'Craterellus Multiplex Cke & Mass an Uncommon and Remarkable Fungus', *Victorian Naturalist*, vol 70, 1954, pp 181–182.

Willis JH, 'Vegetation of the Basalt Plains in Western Victoria', *Proceedings of the Royal Society of Victoria*, vol 77, 1964, pp 397–418.

Willis JH, *Victorian Toadstools and Mushrooms*, Field Naturalists Club of Victoria, 1957.

Wilson BR & Gillett K, *A Field Guide to Australian Shells*, AH & AW Reed, Sydney, 1979.

Wilson F Erasmus, 'Entomological Gleanings from the Otways', *Victorian Naturalist*, vol XLIX, 1932.

Young Tony, *Common Australian Fungi*, New South Wales University Press, Sydney, 1982.

INDEX

Bullhead Minnow 155
Bullkelp (*Durvillea potatorum*) 55, 74, 98
Buprestidae 63
Burchardia umbellata see Milk Maid
burning off 67, 70, 86, 147, 150, 172
Bursaria 27
Bursaria spinosa see Sweet Bursaria
bushfires (Ash Wednesday) 19, 55, 86, 97, 131, 142, 178
bushfires 11, 26, 80, 84–5, 86, 150, 151, 171, 177, 181, 182, 189
butterflies 17, 56–7, 63, 180, 193, 197–8, 199, 206

caddis flies 213
Cakile sp *see* Sea Rocket
Caladenia dilatata see Green-comb Spider Orchid
Caladenia latifolia see Pink Fairy Orchid
Caladenia venusta see Common Spider Orchid
Caleana major see Flying Duck Orchid
Calocephalus brownii see Cushion Bush
Cantharellus lilacinus 112, 113
Cape Otway 1–3, 109, 157, 158, 166, 198, 224
Caper White butterfly (*Anaphaeis java teutonia*) 199
Carpobrotus rossii see Karkalla
Cassinia aculeata see dogwood
Cassytha melantha see Dodder Laurel
Castiarina bremei see jewel beetle
Cattle Egret 142
caves 108, 131, 132, 196
Cellana cf *solida see* limpet
Cellana tramoserica see limpet
Chamaescilla corymbosa see Blue Star
Chamaesipho columna see rock barnacle
Chestnut Teal 146, 155
Chinese Junk caterpillars (*Doratifera* sp) 152–3
chitons 220, 222
Chlorocoma cf *assimilis see* emerald moth
Christmas (Six-spined) Spider (*Gasteracantha minax*) 14, 15
Christmas Bush (*Prostanthera lasianthos*) 23, 83, 217
Chrysanthemoides monilifera see African Boneseed
Chrysolina progressai see beetle
Chrysotricha Skipper (*Hesperilla chrysotricha cyclospila*) 215
cicada (*Cyclochila australasiae*) 19
cicada (*Diemeniana euronotiana*) 18
cicadas 17–18
Cinnabar moth 23
Cirphula pyrrhocnemis 32
Cisseis sp 61, 63
Clavariaceae see Coral Fungi

Clavulinopsis amoena see Coral Fungus
Clavulinopsis miniata see Flame Fungus
Clorophyta *see* seaweeds green
Coast Beard Heath (*Leucopogon parviflorus*) 41, 87, 162, 167, 198, 199
Coast Daisy Bush (*Olearia axillaris*) 132, 134, 166–7
Coast Tea Tree (*Leptospermum laevigatum*) 194, 198
Coastal Wattle (*Acacia longifolia* var *sophorae*) 170
coat-of-mail shell or chiton (*Poneroplax albida*) 220
Coccinella transversalis see ladybird
Collybia elegans see toadstool
Collybia flammulina see Velvet Foot
Coltricia sp 94
Common Beard Heath (*Leucopogon virgatus*) 168
Common Heath (*Epacris impressa*) 31, 58–9, 112, 129–31, 142, 151, 152, 170, 181
Common Spider Orchid (*Caladenia venusta*) 178, 179, 181
Cone Shell (*Conus anemone*) 195
Conus anemone see Cone Shell
Copperhead 49
Coprinus atramentarius see Inky Cap
Coprinus comatus see Shaggy Cap
Coprinus disseminatus see toadstool
Coprinus sp *see* toadstool
Coprosma quadrifida see Prickly Currantbush
Coprosma repens see Looking Glass Plant
Coral Fungi (Clavariaceae) 103–4
Coral Fungus (*Clavulinopsis amoena*) 104
Coral Fungus (*Russula* sp) 95
coral fern (*Gleichenia* sp) 147, 200
Coreidae 41, 43, 215
Correa alba see White Correa
Correa reflexa see correa
Correa reflexa var *nummarifolia* 134
correa (*Correa reflexa*) 134
Cortinarius sp *see* toadstool
Corybas incurvus see Slaty Helmet Orchid
Corybas unguiculatus see Tiny Helmet Orchid
Cosmodes elegans see noctuid moth
Cottony Cushion Scale (*Icerya purchasi*) 215
Cowrie (*Cypraea comptoni*) 195
Crepidotis sp *see* toadstool
Crested Tern 32, 51
crickets 47
Crimson Rosella 96, 176, 217
crow (Australian Raven) 105, 176
Crypostylis subulata see tongue orchid
Cumberland River 127–8, 212, 213
Cup Fungus 94

cup moth (*Doratifera* sp) 152–3
Cupressus macrocarpa see Monterey Cypress
Cushion Bush (*Calocephalus brownii*) 107, 132, 134
Cyathea australis see Rough Tree Fern
Cyathea cunninghamii see Slender Tree Fern
Cyathea X Marescens see Skirted Tree Fern
Cyclochila australasiae see cicada
Cypraea comptoni see Cowrie

Damsel fly (*Austrolestes analis*) 201
Damsel fly (*Austrolestes leda*) 200
Daviesia brevifolia see Leafless Bitter-pea
day-flying moth (*Epicoma contristis*) 214
Death Cap (*Amanita phalloides*) 117
Deep Creek 222, 223
Delias aganippe see Wood White butterfly
Demons Bluff 168
Diaea sp 215
Diamma bicolor see Blue Ant
Dianella longifolia see Pale Flax Lily flower
Dicksonia antarctica see Soft Tree Fern
dieback (*Phytophthera cinnamomi*) 208–9
Diemeniana euronotiana see cicada
digger wasp (*Pison* sp) 167
Dillwynia cinerascens see Grey Parrot-pea
Dindymus versicolor see harlequin bugs
Dinosaur Cove 49–50
Dipodium punctatum see Hyacinth Orchid
Dispar compacta see Dispar Skipper
Dispar Skipper (*Dispar compacta*) 57
Disphyma crassifolium ssp *Clavellatum see* pigface (Rounded Noon Flower)
Diuris corymbosa see Wallflower Orchid
Diuris palustris see Swamp Diuris
Diuris sp *see* donkey orchid
Diuris sulphurea see Tiger Orchid
Dodder Laurel (*Cassytha melantha*) 99
Dog's Tooth Moss 14
Dogwood (*Cassinia aculeata*) 83, 216
donkey orchid (*Diuris* sp) 173
Donnysa Skipper butterfly (*Hesperilla donnysa delos*) 207
Doodia caudata see Small Rasp Fern
Doratifera sp *see* Chinese Junk caterpillars
Dotted Sun Orchid (*Thelymitra ixioides*) 180, 181
Douglas Fir (*Pseudotsuga menziesii*) 23, 134
dragonfly (*Hemianax papuensis*) 183